CLANDESTINE: THE FALLEN ANGEL SAGA

For Regina Miller, Linda Kingery, and Jay Swisher.

Made with love.
Made out of love.
Because of love.

CLANDESTINE: THE FALLEN ANGEL SAGA

The Fallen Angel Saga

ARTHUR J. MCWILLIAMS

Arthur J. McWilliams

Contents

I

Michael

The Archangel Michael, High Commander of Heaven, turns around in the Parisian hotel lobby and blinks. He isn't sure where he's supposed to be, but the note in his pocket says here. Michael received a location, and a time, by way of a message carrier. He is here on time, but his companion for the evening is late.

He is wearing a silver suit with yellow accents that goes well with his dark brown oxfords and his tortoiseshell glasses that he only wears on earth. Not that another angel would not recognize him, but he's trying to blend in. His blonde hair is longer than ear length currently, but he has it tied back on his head to keep his face free of the strands.

He rechecks his pocket watch. He sighs and slips it back into the small pocket of his waistcoat. He is waiting in the lobby of the L'hôtel Eden. It's late September, and it's reasonably warm in Paris, France. The year of our Lord is 1984, and it's been over a year since he's been back to earth.

"Is there any way I can help you, sir? You seem to be lost." A kind woman asks in French, then English, as she comes closer. She wears a black pantsuit with a small silver name tag that says, Marie. Michael is fascinated by the fetching red scarf around her neck. He likes red. It reminds him of the person he's waiting on.

"I am waiting for my companion. We are meet-ing for a-" Michael has to think about what they're doing. The human term is in there somewhere, in his mind. He nods with a beaming smile once he recalls it. "We have a date, but they're late, it seems." His French is poor, but he fumbles through communicating with her.

"Would you prefer to wait at the bar? We have a wonderful drink selection." She gestures to the left. "I'm sure your ....companion." She looks like she's inferring something. "Could see you there." Michael scans her mind. She's scared of the optics of a well-dressed man waiting for a prostitute in her Hotel. This is not what she wants for her Hotel. Michael has to sigh because that's not why he's here, either.

"I am fine," He smooths down his tie. "Thank you. I will wait here for my date." He smiles at her and manages a slight change in her perception. Her head cants as his mind invites her to look again. He makes her believe there is nothing wrong with waiting for a date in a hotel lobby. A minor miracle they use on humans is to make them forget they saw one of them or walk away. After all, this keeps them safe.

"Very well, sir, enjoy your date." She smiles and moves on to the next patron, who looks lost. Michael's eyes watch her walk. From the back, he notes the red soles on her shoes. Like the red scarf, it contrasts deeply with everything else and keeps his eyes as she goes.

Beelzebub appears at his side, looking at her as Michael seems to be, "She's cute." He looks handsome, hair long and stringy around his face and eyes. "Not quite my type, but cute anyhow."

Michael turns to him, his voice frustrated. "You're late." He doesn't want to talk about the woman. The demon, predictably, is dressed all in black. The red pocket square in the front pocket of his suit catches his eye. Had he shown up like that, or had he added it to match the woman to get Michael's attention? Whatever the reason, it worked. "Were there problems?" Michael forces himself to ask as his eyes roam up and down the demon's attire.

"Got held up, can't help it if the boss needs me." He shrugs. "Dinner first?" Beelzebub gives him a pull on his elbow, and they walk together.

"I would like that, yes." Michael smiles, falling in step with him. "I'm glad you came." Michael is always terrible when it comes to small talk. "You look well." The following words tumble out, "I've missed you."

The ruby eyes meet his own, and he beams a bright smile, "Thank you, me too, and after you." Beelzebub motions him to the Hotel's restaurant, and they walk together. His answers are usually curt like this in public.

"Should anyone see us, Bee-" Michael looks all around.

"No one is going to see us, Mike. Calm down." He walks up to the host. "Table for two under the name Benjamin Hive. One of the private booths, please."

The girl looks down at the host menu, eyes glazed over as she nods blankly. She gathers two menus and a wine list. "This way, gentlemen." They follow her back to a small booth where they sit. The curtains around them are closed. "Enjoy your meal."

"You don't have to manipulate their minds." Michael sighs. "I would have been happy to wait."

"Come on, Michael, live a little." Beelzebub doesn't look ashamed at all. "It would have been a fifty-minute wait. I'm not the type to wait, and besides, what do you think you did with that nice woman in the lobby, hmm? You didn't have to do that either, but you did. The red scarf, the heels, thinking of me?"

"It's been a long time since you presented such femininity." He points toward the lobby, "That was little more than casting a mirror, something all of us do. Acting in such a manner as you did with the host is taking advantage, and it's a completely different scenario." Michael sighs before scrubbing his face with his hands. "I am sorry I haven't been able to get away as of late; things are ... busy upstairs, and Gabriel's been all over me."

"Hopefully, he's good in the sack," Beelzebub smirks.

"He's my brother." Michael shakes his head. "That's not-"

"Calm down. I was trying to be funny." Beelzebub smiles as the waiter appears, setting down glasses of water. Beelzebub waves a hand, and the waiter nods and leaves. "I ordered your favorite and some wine."

"The fish."

"The fish is your favorite, at least I can remember." Beelzebub scrunches up his nose. He smiles, "you're not sleeping. How long has it been? Since you had even the slightest nap?" Michael isn't sure how the demon can know that.

"Three months." It's true. He's exhausted.

"You'd better enjoy that fish, so I can get you into a bed." The handsome Prince has told him he hates the smell of fish occasionally. Michael wonders why, but he's never asked, but Beelzebub always seems to indulge Michael with what he wants.

Wine comes first to them, and they murmur about what is going on with their work. However, redacted that conversation may come, Michael is open to it. Beelzebub says his fellow royals ask questions about why he's often away; he's running out of excuses. Though their rendezvous are so far apart, it's a wonder why anyone would ask questions.

Michael admits the same things are going on in Heaven. They will need to space their meetings further apart, or there will be problems on both sides. They agree to work on a schedule to suit their needs. Communication is complex between them, they have set up postage boxes on earth and send messages via human courier, but even their weekly notes may be too risky.

Dinner is nothing to linger over; they eat their food, drink their wine, and Beelzebub manages the check to Micahel's protests.

Beelzebub doesn't want to waste the time they have and teleports them to the top floor of the Hotel. They stand outside a pair of Ivory french doors. "I think this will do." Beelzebub nods at the doors with a beaming smile.

"What is this room?" They've always just gotten a small room on the lower floor of the Hotel.

The key slides into the door slowly, and Beelzebub turns the tumbler over before righting the key and pulling it back out. The door opens, and he holds it open for Michael to walk ahead. "Penthouse." Beelzebub smiles, "Thought I should go all out before we have to be apart for another year." Beelzebub is delighted with the main room.

"It might be longer than a year," Michael admits. "I want to ensure we have time to get everything done we desire."

Beelzebub turns his fingers grabbing to pull Michael's tie off. "We have plenty of time, commander," He says softly.

"High Commander." Michael shucks out of his jacket and lays it over a chair. He pulls out his notebook and pen, setting them down on the table. Michael unlatches his watch and lays it beside the book. "Is my official title."

"Is it?" Beelzebub chuckles, teasing. He pulls the tie out from Michael's shirt collar tossing it down to the ground.

Beelzebub lays out his cigarette case and lighter. Michael's hands rub up Beelzebub's neck to cradle his head. The kiss is firm and deep. "Bee-" Michael says his name fervently against his lips. "I missed you." His fingers grab greedily against the shorter man's shirt.

"We can take our time, High Commander." Beelzebub kisses him again and bites his lip. "We have plenty." Meaning time.

"Your Highness." Michael moans softly and pulls Beelzebub flush against him. "Get undressed. I want to see you, touch you."

Beelzebub chuckles. "Sure." He pushes Michael to step back to take his coat off. "Do you touch yourself up there in Heaven thinking about me?"

Michael has to seal his eyes and swallow, but he nods; he cannot lie to him. "Often, more often than I would rather wish to admit." His fingers undo buttons, starting at his neck and going down before Beelzebub's dark hands force his fingers away. "Bee-"

"Quiet, I like that. I'm up there somehow in Heaven, even if it's only in your thoughts." Beelzebub continues the buttons down and leans up to kiss Michael deeply.

"And prayers."

Beelzebub groans loudly at Michael's sincerity.

"Shut up before I gag you." Such tiny deft fingers make quick work of those pearly white buttons. Michael marvels at Beelzebub's determination.

Michael's brow rises, curious about the statement. "Gag me? You can't be serious."

"Oh, I'm serious, very." Beelzebub smiles as the last button comes free. He pushes the shirt over Michael's shoulders, and the angel pulls it off, letting it fall to the floor. Michael grabs his neck again, kissing him, pulling at the demon's black shirt. Beelzebub hisses. "Don't you dare? This shirt is my good shirt." Beelzebub argues and steps back to take it off one small button at a time. "The last one you tore all the buttons off of, and after, I never thought I'd hear the end of it." Beelzebub rolls his eyes.

"From whom?" Michael chuckles. "Do you have someone who mends your shirts?"

"I do. I am a prince, after all, probably the same immortal tailor who does yours?"

Michael looks down at his shirt on the floor. "Ah, Frigg."

"Her." Beelzebub tosses the shirt aside and pulls his belt from its loops, tossing it down. "Come here."

They undress, leaving a trail of clothing to the king-sized bed behind two double doors. "I want you." Michael picks up the more petite man and carries him a few feet to the bed to lay him out. "God in Heaven, you are so beautiful."

"God stays in Heaven. This is you and me," Beelzebub smirks. "Fuck me." He mutters as if things are suddenly dawning on him.

"As is my intention," a hand ghosts over Beelzebub's shoulder. "But my intention is truly to love you completely." Michael smiles, and they kiss again. Beelzebub's fingers trace his face, and Michael wonders why it doesn't burn, these delicate touches from the damned.

"You're too sentimental."

Beelzebub kisses him again, and when they part, those blood-red eyes stare up at him. "I love you," Michael murmurs. "So much." he can't help but say it. Has to.

Beelzebub nods, acknowledging but never responding to that. He has never been one to respond to that, but there is something there, Michael thinks. In the softness of the ruby gaze. A feeling they share that they both understand. "Come on." Beelzebub crawls backward on the bed to the pillows laying himself out. "I have been waiting for over a year for this." Michael obediently obliges him.

It's still very early the following day when Michael wakes up. Beelzebub is sleeping across his chest, an arm wrapped around him slackly. Michael leans down, kissing his forehead, "I love you." He murmurs, lifting that hand to set it aside to roll slowly to get out from under the Prince, who does not stir.

Michael stands, grabbing his boxers and pulling them to the table near the window. He looks out at the sky and the quiet street below at this early hour. A few cars roll by; a drunk stumbles down the road quietly. He looks up to see birds on one of the nearby rooftops. He likes the view; being high up makes him feel more comfortable.

"Something wrong?" Beelzebub asks.

Michael whirls around to see Beelzebub sitting on the edge of the bed, lighting a cigarette. "I didn't mean to wake you, Beelzebub. I was curious if Heaven hasn't burned to the ground in my absence."

"Has it ever?" Beelzebub takes a draw off the

cigarette and blows the smoke out his nose. "Honestly?"

"No." He returns to the bed and sits beside the demon, offering the cigarette. Michael can only shake his head and hold up a hand in decline. "Gabriel usually has everything well in hand." He looks out at the city.

"Then why are you so far away?" Beelzebub asks, touching his knuckles to Michael's cheek. "You're supposed to be here with me."

"Dunno." Michael turns to him and smiles. "I don't do this often."

"Fuck a demon?" Beelzebub turns to the side table, tapping his cigarette, and an ashtray appears to collect the ashes. "Get laid? Leave Heaven?"

"All those things, but mostly taking time for me," Michael murmurs, unphased by Beelzebub's tone or phrasing.

"Perhaps you should do it more often," Beelzebub says with a smile. "Next weekend."

"I can't," Michael says. "We- we can't. Getting away for even a day is a tax on me. I am already so far behind. Setting me back further will not endear my people to allow me to take time off like this. I shouldn't have in the first place. I have a duty."

"It's over a year between when we can see one another, and-" Beelzebub shuts up rather quickly, cigarette finding his lips as if to safeguard himself from speaking more. It's not been Michael's experience that Beelzebub would censor himself.

"You want more." Michael can guess what he wants, but making those promises is hard.

"Don't you?" Beelzebub asks incredulously.

"I- yes." Michael sighs. "Of course I do, but neither of our sides will think what we are doing is okay. Bee, this is dangerous." He frowns. "If Gabriel ever found out, or Ariel, there would be Hell to pay."

Beelzebub nods, "What time is it?"

"About four in the morning," Michael says, looking at the bedside clock.

"You have to leave at dawn," Beelzebub yawns deeply. "Come back to bed." He snuffs the cigarette out in the ashtray and rolls back into the bed. "If I only have you for a few more hours, I want to make the best of it."

"Agreed." Michael turns, crawling over him. "I love you."

"Good." Beelzebub smirks, "Now do as I say." Beelzebub points at the pillow beside his head.

Michael can only nod his agreement, and he turns the demon's head. He leans down, planning to kiss a line up his neck to his small pale ears. Michael freezes his thumb, moving hair away from the back of his ear. "Bee?" His eyes lock on a mark behind Beelzebub's left ear, which he has never noticed.

"Hmmm?" Beelzebub is kissing his hand. "What?" Michael sucks in a tight breath as Beelzebub bites the webbed flesh between his thumb and index finger.

"You have a horseshoe shape in your hairline." His breath is soft and nearly stolen. The realization is a heartbreaking discovery for Michael, his destiny now staring him in the face.

Beelzebub stops and reaches back to touch the mark. "Yeah, I know."

"I have a similar mark," Michael says, turning to lift the hair behind his ear.

Beelzebub turns to him, suddenly looking. "You're War."

"What does that make you?" Michael asks.

"My demonic trait is Gluttony," Beelzebub shrugs and shakes his head. "Fa- The Boss says that most likely makes me famine, as I would steal all the food away from people," he says softly and sits down. "When it's all over, I guess it's gonna be you, me, Death, and whoever is Pestilence."

Michael swallows and nods. "Our destiny, it seems, is already interconnected."

"I guess so." Beelzebub nods. "I don't know who Pestilence is. I felt you were the horseman of War, and it seemed only appropriate."

"Sickness, disease." Michael muses. "I wouldn't even know where to start looking..."

"Dunno." Beelzebub frowns. "Guess that kills the mood." He leans back on the pillows and sighs. "Look, whoever it is, it would be a healer, most likely, or someone who can't get sick."

"A spreader." Michael says, "A carrier." He lays down beside Beelzebub and pulls him closer.

"A human?" Beelzebub shrugs. "Or a Hybrid." He rolls to face Michael and touches his cheek.

"That's a definite possibility." Michael shrugs and looks past Beelzebub while he is trying to consider.

Beelzebub sighs, "Must we discuss it now?"

Michael looks down into those red eyes. Shaking his head, he pulls Beelzebub closer to him. "No, we needn't." He kisses the Prince's forehead and holds him tightly to his chest.

II

Beelzebub

Beelzebub is tying his tie in the bathroom mirror, a cigarette hanging from his lip, and sunlight streaming in the windows. "You're horrible at that," Michael observes, coming into the bathroom and setting an ashtray down on the counter. "Turn."

"We usually have valets who dress us." He says. "It's only when I'm off with you that I have to do all this myself."

"A Valet, huh? What's their name?" Michael asks with a smile in the mirror.

"Hauster, he's a Duke." Beelzebub rolls his eyes. "Fourth in line for the throne."

"Interesting." Beelzebub turns and watches the taller angel fix the tie with ease. "There." Michael sets his collar, but his angelic fingers linger on his neck. "You can't go back to Hell looking like Hell now, can you?"

Beelzebub shrugs, turn to the mirror, checks his face, and fixes his hair. "Gotta meeting with fa-," There's a snap correction. "the boss in a few hours." He rolls his eyes looking away. "Maybe I can nap on my throne for a bit. I'll be fine."

"Do you have one? A throne?"

Beelzebub nods, "Made of dark stone, red cush-ions; I'll bring a photo of it next time to show you."

"I would have thought Lucifer would be the one on a throne." Michael shrugs. "Seeing as he's the king and all."

"My fa-" this keeps happening; he keeps mis-speaking, "Look, the boss has more important things that he's doing. I rule Hell, and I'm in charge. He isn't, not anymore." He doesn't need to let on that he calls Lucifer Father or his mother's existence.

"Ah, so you *are* my counterpart then?" Michael smiles. There's an inflection in how he says it, like he's just discovered something new.

"Indeed, and how is it?" Beelzebub taps his cigarette in the ashtray, "How is it you and I cannot find time for ourselves when we're running the entire show? Someone needs to explain that to me. Cause I'd like to know the damned answer."

"There are too many people watching what we are doing. If I spend more than a day or so away from Heaven, Gabriel will ask questions." Michael shrugs. "Raphael too."

Beelzebub frowns, leaning on the counter. "And what explanation do you owe them?"

"They are my brothers." Said as if he couldn't think to hurt them. "The generals directly under me, and if they are asking questions, the others are too: Ariel, Cassiel, Jophiel." Michael seems upset by that last one. "He's a gossip hound, that one."

"They're not your keepers," Beelzebub says firmly. "I told my brother I was coming to earth, and I came." He gestures around, "I wanted to be here. I made that happen."

"You were also late." Michael teases, but Beelzebub likes how the light sparkles in his golden eyes when he does so.

"Yes, I made it here, didn't I?" Michael leans

down, meeting his lips in answer. The kiss is so good that Beelzebub nearly loses his balance. "Back in the bed; I want you again." It tumbles out before the Prince can recant it.

"I can't," Michael laments. "I have to go." It sounds to Beelzebub like he's still trying to convince himself of that one.

"Fuck them." Beelzebub says, "One more hour, stay with me." He's not begging, no, not really; a prince wouldn't beg. Would he?

"I-" Michael looks frustrated now. "I can't, my love." Beelzebub lets him go and walks out of the bathroom. When Michael appears, he grabs his watch off the bedside counter and slips it on his wrist. "Bee, come on."

Beelzebub's eyes flash deep red. He lowers his head and shakes off the headache of being called home. "Shit." He mutters.

"Are you alright?" Michael asks with deep concern.

"Yes, of course, I am; it's fine." Beelzebub turns with a smile, putting on his brave face. "I know. I have to go too." He shrugs. "I just thought- maybe, but we're out of time for today, it seems." His eyes flash again, and he raises his hand to hide the change in brightness. His father must be screaming his name.

Michael comes forward, taking his hand to twist it away, kissing him hard. "Tonight, book the room again. I'll get Ariel to cover my appointments."

"Do you mean that?" Beelzebub looks at him, and his voice is a breath of awe.

"Of course, my love, but just this once. It will be a while before I can afford to do something like this again." Beelzebub hates the sound of that.

"Deal," he nods, "but we get room service." There is no room to debate it. "I must have room service."

"What's room service?" Michael asks curiously.

Beelzebub smiles, "You'll see. Go on; we'll meet back here tonight, say six?"

Michael nods. "Closer to seven, maybe eight, but I'll be here."

"Good." Beelzebub nods and watches the angel gather his things and teleport out of the room. Beelzebub rubs at his chest to push away the ache that he feels. He has to handle that feeling of loss; it won't serve him.

Beelzebub cracks his neck and adjusts his tie

one last time before he does the same, appearing in the great throne room. His eyes look around, the thrones are empty, and this is where he had been summoned to. "And where have you been?!" Beelzebub flinches and turns around to meet her blue eyes standing in the doorway.

"Mother-" Beelzebub holds up his hands.

"Your father has been calling on you. Where were you?" Lilith comes to him to straighten his hair and his lapels. "You're an absolute sight." She smooths out wrinkles on his jacket before buttoning it in front of his shirt.

"I was upstairs." Beelzebub smiles. "Took a night off, gonna take tonight off too." he pulls his cigarette case out and taps it against the heel of his hand. "What's going on?"

"You need to see your father before he removes Leviathan's head from his shoulders." She insists. "Go on."

Beelzebub frowns, "What did Levi do?"

"Your brother? Nothing. Your father is just in a piss poor mood, and it's because you're not here to handle things." Lilith's eyes narrow, "He's not happy, that's for damned sure, and it has to do with you running off yesterday."

Beelzebub shrugs. "I was meeting someone. I do that, you know, have meetings with people."

"Make sure your dalliances don't come before the throne, or your father will remove you from it." He meets her eyes, and she smiles at him and softens. "Handsome." She fixes his hair further. "Go to him. Be repentant." She advises.

"Yes, mother." He bows his head. "I will."

"I will make sure Asmodeus can take over for you tonight." she smiles and cups his face, lifting it to look into his eyes. "It's about time with you." She smiles so brightly. "I'm happy that you've found it."

"About time for what?" Beelzebub turns, "Found what, mother?"

A kiss on his forehead, and she walks off. Beelzebub sighs and pushes into the main hall, where Lucifer is seated at their dining table with a glass of wine. His brother Leviathan stands beyond the table, hand on his sword." Where were you?" Lucifer's tone is dark.

"On earth, with an angel." He shrugs. "Why else do I go other than to get laid?" He knows he cannot lie to this demon, Lucifer, his demonic father, and king, though he does not have to offer the entirety of his truth.

"Leviathan, you're dismissed."

"Father, Brother." Leviathan bows to both before exiting a door on the far side of the room.

When they are alone, Lucifer says, "We have a problem." He turns his red eyes to Beelzebub, who nods, letting Lucifer know he can go on. "A demon destroyed an angel; Heaven wants answers." He motions a hand to an open folder.

"Which demon killed which angel?" Beelzebub walks up, putting his silver case into his jacket pocket. He stands still, waiting.

Lucifer pushes the papers on the table over to him, "Nergal, one of yours, I think," Lucifer shakes his head. "Killed an angel, Heaven says he claims it was an accident, but we received a holy summons to the Empty Realm to talk terms." The Empty Realm is a small pocket world where angels and demons could both exist safely; it was used for almost all negotiations and was held in control by Death. This was all well and good. It kept the appearance of balance on both sides.

"Which angel?" Beelzebub keeps his stance loose as he thumbs through the papers.

"An angel named Mathias." Lucifer explains, "A watcher." He takes his wine glass and takes a drink.

Beelzebub turns around. "Where is Nergal now?"

"Being held in the Empty Realm by Heaven in a cage so I am told. Heaven would prosecute with Raguel and Phanuel, their Justice and Judgement angels."

Beelzebub rolls his eyes. "Will Heaven allow demonic council?"

"They had better." Lucifer sits back.

"I will speak with Lucas immediately-"

Lucifer looks to be considering things; Beelzebub's eyes flit back from his father to the papers. "Beelzebub," He meets his father's eyes. "You will never again ignore my summons. Am I clear?" Lucifer says calmly, rolling the wine glass between the palms of his hands. "You will return the MOMENT I summon you, or I will force you back here myself." Beelzebub knows that Lucifer would have to unhitch his powers from their mother, he does not see it happening, but he cannot ignore the threat.

"Yes, father. You've made yourself clear." Beelzebub bows are far lower than necessary. "My king."

Lucifer walks away, footfalls echoing back into the royal household's chambers. "Shit." Beelzebub lets out a breath he hadn't realized he'd held for so long. He braces his hand on his chest. "Fuck." He turns, gathering up all the documentation before pushing it into the folder and leaving out the door Leviathan had exited out of; he has to find Lucas, fast.

III

Michael

Michael is grabbed by the arm the moment he's back in The Heavenly halls. "Raph?"

"Where have you been?" Raphael clutches his arm tighter and speaks in a whisper, "Mathias was destroyed."

"What?" Michael has to do a double-take, stopping himself. "What do you mean?"

"A demon known as Nergal killed him." He sighs, "Gabriel is on the warpath. We're holding the demon in the Empty Realm in a warded cell. He's going to stand trial."

"On whose authority?" Michael demands instantly.

"Gabriel's. You weren't here, and he had the authority to make that call." Raphael says, "Listen to me. Gabriel's already got Raguel And Phanuel ready to head to the Empty Realm right now. There's more than enough to win this case against him."

"A trial." Michael sighs. "Has Hell been contacted? Do they know what is going on?" Their feet start walking and they continue down the hallway, Raphael still at his side.

"Yes, per our treaties, we informed Lucifer the moment we took the demon into custody, Hell has the option to supply the demon council or to leave him to our mercy," Raphael says looking at his notes.

"Knowing Gabriel, there would be no mercy," Michael accepts what Raphael is saying, "I want Gabriel in my office in ten minutes. Make it happen, please."

"Of course." Raphael teleports away. Michael teleports straight to his office, writes a brief letter, and seals it before using a miracle to make it vanish and put it into the bag of a courier on earth who will see it to its destination.

Gabriel smiles brightly, opens the door without a knock, and strides right in. "We're going to see that demon drown in holy water, brother." Michael has never seen Gabriel so happy, "Oh it's gonna be a good show!"

"Good morning to you too, Gabriel." Michael turns to a file cabinet and pulls out a few documents. He lays them out on his desk. "I hear you had an eventful evening."

"Let's go. It's perfect timing!" Gabriel motions to the door. "We can finish this now." He's beaming with pride.

"I have questions first," Michael says, opening his file and sitting down.

"Michael, please, it's an obvious case in Heaven's favor!" Gabriel is insistent.

"Then explain it to me. If it's clear cut, so be it, but we can't have Hell thinking we didn't cover our bases." Michael opens the file and pulls out a few treaties that he and Beelzebub had commissioned. "We have to do this right, and if we don't, we risk a lot if we're wrong."

Gabriel sits down and leans back, "I guess Mathias and Nergal were both acquiring souls in the same area of America, maybe. That was my initial thought."

"You guess?"

"I wasn't there, Michael. I can only go by what we know." He says, "Which until I get up there and question Nergal more is very little."

"So this is a territorial spat?"

"Spat, Mathias was killed, Micahel." Gabriel leans forward. "This wasn't just a spat. What happened last night," he points his finger onto the paperwork, "is murder."

"Ok, so then, what happened?" Michael lowers the treaty and pulls out a map to unfold.

"As far as we can tell, Nergal says that Mathias was in the demonic territory and was infringing upon his right to see his daughter."

"And who gave you that information?" Michael levels his eyes on Gabriel.

"The two sentries that brought him in, Solus and Lincoln." Gabriel shrugs, "Sol said he kept going on about his daughter."

"So they weren't collecting souls." Another

confirmation of why Gabriel is just not suited to bureaucracy. "A hybrid." Michael frowns. "His daughter is a hybrid?"

"Yes. And from what else Solus said, Nergal thought he was being watched over, well Mathias is a watcher; that's his job."

"Demons wouldn't know that, Gabriel." Michael says, "But go on-"

"Fine, but he wasn't in Demonic territories like he claims. He was in Heavenly ones." Gabriel shrugs. "Hard to tell. It's very close to a territorial line." Gabriel points down at the map, "though I wish Mathias were here to give his side of the story."

"The treaties with Hell about The Watchers watching over demons is very clear." Micahel says, "And Mathias would have known he was to stay away from them. Watchers are meant to watch humans. What was his assignment? Who was he watching?"

"He was watching Negal's daughter." Gabriel uses a miracle and offers Michael a file folder. "Quilla, but this Nergal got in the way, looks like."

"Not familiar with Quilla or her father." Michael turns the file over.

"Quilla was an Incan Goddess, well pretended to be." He reaches across to point out something on a report for Michael. "She didn't age, and humans worshiped her for years, hoping to have her youth somehow."

"We didn't get involved because-"

"Well, she's a hybrid. She's half-human, half-demon." Gabriel says, shrugging. "Not our purview, and at that time, we were more concerned with the progression of Religion in the eastern part of the world."

Michael lays the folder down. "And who assigned Mathias to watch Quilla?"

"Not sure you would call it assigned, but it was indirect, I can almost assure you," Gabriel leans forward. "We have been conducting a hybrid headcount. After all, they are immortal beings." He says, "It would be nice to know just exactly how many are left."

Michael nods. "Is Quilla being held? Are we allowing her to stay near her father, and did she see anything?"

"We're unsure, but she's a demon spawn. She's not ours to question." Gabriel shakes his head, "If hell wants to let her move into the Empty for the trial that's their business."

"Well, her testimony might make a difference in this case. See if Phanuel or Raguel will want to take a stab at finding her first."

Gabriel stands and heads for the door, "Can I ask you something?"

Michael is taking notes, he doesn't look up, "Of course, what is it?"

"Where were you last night?"

Michael smirks but doesn't look up. "I was in Paris to attend a sword exposition." That's true. There was one; he had a ticket. Gabriel didn't need to know if he attended. Michael always had a cover for his meetings with the one he loved.

"Find anything good in Paris?" What an easy question to answer.

"Nothing better than what God gave me." Which could stand for any number of things.

Gabriel beams a smile, "Exactly, so I don't understand why you even go." He exits the room, and Michael lets out a sigh and leans back in his seat.

In his office later, Raphael sits across from him.

"The hybrid has arrived at the meeting place along with the demonic council."

"What is the counselor's name?"

"This missive from Beelzebub says the councilman is named Lucas; he is a Duke." Raphael beams, "I don't know what a Duke is..."

"Just under the royal family, I believe. Lucas may have unlimited access to their client." Michael makes a note on his sheet. "And Quilla. She is allowed visits with both the demonic councilor and her father."

"Of course." Raphael agrees, making another note. "The entirety of the royal family of Hell wishes to attend."

"The whole family?" Raphael nods at him, "Lucifer too?" Michael looks up his voice a little curious, none had seen him since the fall, nor laid eyes on him.

"No, just the Crown Prince Beelzebub, Prince Leviathan, and Princess Asmodeus." Raphael passes over another sheet. "Regulations for their seating and their pronouncements." Raphael sighs. "I miss him too."

"He made his choices, and he and his people are living with them." Michael shakes his head.

"They Called it a way of Balance." Raphael sighs.

"I know what God called it," Michael says softly and takes a look at the seating chart. "This is all very easily accommodatable." he nods "make it happen, Chairs for You, Gabriel, and myself in a similar fashion," he suggests. "We can keep up with that for appearance's sake."

Raphael hands over another form. "Alright, and next things next, Gabriel is prepping to bring a tank of Holy water-"

Michael has to drop his folder down; all he can manage is a frown. "No, we do not make judgments like that, if he is found guilty, Gabriel can fetch it per the by-laws, but we're not walking into a trial with that sort of bias right out in front." He points his pen to Raphael. "He knows better."

"He's angry." Raphael says as if that should excuse it, "You can't blame him for being upset that one of our angels is dead. Cassiel is distraught. It was one of his."

Michael sets his papers down and sighs. "Raph, I'm not blaming him for being upset. I'm just not wanting Hell to think we're jumping the gun. We have treaties like this for a reason. The war with

Hell will never be over; we're simply in a lasting ceasefire."

Raphael looks at him. "You're hurting over this."

"We've lost an angel, brother. Facing Hell will not be easy. It never is." He doesn't say why. He glances at his watch and sighs. "Like they said Balance." Michael nods "It's all a balancing act and Gabriel has about as much finesse as a snake trying to hug a mouse."

Raphael stands and comes to sit beside him on the sofa he's on. "Mike, you're stressed out. The trial isn't for two days. Do you need some time for yourself?" Raphael pats his back gently. "This is a lot and you're trying to go to war with all of it." Michael can't deny the accuracy of the statement.

He buckles finally knowing exactly what he wants, "Do you think Ariel could take over my appointments?"

"I could ask her. If not, I'll do it. I'll get Gabriel to stand down a little bit, and we'll all meet for lunch tomorrow to discuss."

Michael nods, "Thank you."

Raphael smiles. "What are best friends for, huh? Go on." He waves a hand. "Get out of here and clear your head." He waves a hand around, "I mean last night was a business trip wasn't it?"

"More personal really, I was off looking at swords. I didn't find one I liked," Michael says, speaking more truth than actual facts. "How do you plan to handle all this?"

"I'll handle things with Ariel like we always do, and also comfort Cassie. He's so upset." He nods. "We'll manage, we have Gabriel too."

"Thank you, brother."

"Go before Gabriel gets back." Raphael teases. Michael smiles as he vanishes.

IV

Beelzebub

It's late when the door on the Penthouse opens inward. The sound makes Beelzebub look up from the scrawled note quickly. Beelzebub stands from the bed, wiping at his eyes a moment before clearing his throat and moving to the door silently, the message forgotten on the duvet. Michael, it's Michael who's come into the Penthouse.

Beelzebub silently watches him through the crack in the bedroom's french doors holding his breath. He's gotten a note Michael had sent to the hotel, sure he wasn't coming. Michael lifts the lid on the silver tea set. The food was gone by the time

Michael showed up. That said, Beelzebub should have waited, but he couldn't. He was never good at waiting when food was around.

Beelzebub opens the doors and smirks, speaking up. "You're here." He tries to keep the surprise out of his voice, but he doesn't seem to manage. He stands in just his black dress shirt and waistcoat. He's left his jacket and tie on the bed with the note. "I got a note from the front desk." he thumbs over his shoulder.

"I wasn't sure if I would be able to come." Michael stands straight and sets the lid on the empty plate. "I don't even know if I can stay, what-" He swallows, "With everything that's happening." Beelzebub watches him unbutton his jacket and slowly remove it from his shoulders, looking around. His hand goes next to his tie to pull it loose; it hangs down around his neck.

Beelzebub leans on the door, stuffing his hands in his pockets. "This isn't going to be easy, not for anyone, least of all the two of us."

"We've lost an angel," Michael says firmly. "That's not acceptable, and you have to understand that."

"And you're holding one of mine, who will

probably die." Beelzebub says softly, "You have to consider where I'm standing-"

"He was in the wrong place-" Michael argues.

"What?" Beelzebub walks forward, interrupting, pulling his hands free to gesture. "At the wrong time?" Beelzebub points angrily at Michael and suddenly pockets the hand.

"He was seeing his child." Michael informs, "A hybrid known as Quilla. She's recently had a baby, and he's a grandfather."

Beelzebub pauses, "I didn't know that. That wasn't in our files." He turns around for a moment to think.

"We just found out for ourselves."

"That doesn't make it better, Michael!" Beelzebub frowns.

"I won't get in a row with you, not here, not now," Michael looks away. "I should go-" He's glancing around like he's looking for something. "We must stop these clandestine meetings-" He doesn't sound like he means that part, breaking something in Beelzebub.

"No!" Beelzebub says a little too desperately. He gathers himself better, smoothing down his waistcoat. "Stay. Look, Michael, I'm sorry. Nergal is part of my own Legion. If he dies, I'll get the great honor of feeling that death. Forgive me for being afraid of feeling that sensation again because I have felt it many times, and it never gets better." Beelzebub bites out, turning to look at the wall for a moment.

"You're his Host?" Michael asks curiously, his voice taking on a sympathetic tone. "You've felt their destructions before? Your body of Demons?"

"It's what we call a Legion. But yes, it's something like that." Beelzebub says softly. "When a legionnaire comes to hell, we feel their birth, and when a legionnaire dies, we have to feel that death also." Beelzebub walks over to the minibar and pours a drink. He can't keep Michael here, and this is hard enough as it is. "It's nothing. Go if you're going-"

"You asked me to stay." Beelzebub nods in agreement; he had, "was this act-"Michael sounds unsure, "ordered, by the Crown-"

Beelzebub turns and barks in return, "Of course, it wasn't ordered by the Crown! I am the Crown!" Beelzebub takes a moment to calm himself, take a deep breath and let it out. "We have a cease-fire."

He has never broken it with any of his orders. "It still stands, does it not?" He shakes his head, reaching up to rub at his eyes. "Fuck."

"We do have a cease-fire. It stands." Michael agrees. Beelzebub is looking away, but he can hear the footsteps. He can feel the firm hand on his shoulder. "We do." It is more of a grounding statement to reinforce how they both feel.

Beelzebub lifts the glass he poured and downs the amber liquid inside. He makes a face and lifts the bottle. "Bourbon." He sighs and sets it down. "Never a good Cognac when I need one."

Michael's arms wrap around him. "I'll call the front desk and have some brought up." Michael's chin rests on his shoulder, and they stand there for an eternity.

"It's fine, you don't have to do that," Beelzebub shakes his head, "What do we do?"

"I don't know," Michael murmurs. "I suppose we let the process go forward." A pause. "That's all we can do." A kiss presses into his neck.

"Trust the process?" Beelzebub asks softly.

"Trust the process." Michael agrees, kissing again.

"What happens if this breaks everything apart?"

Beelzebub asks, hands firmly leaning on the bar now, head down. The ache is so hard to fight.

Beelzebub can feel Michael's hands back away from him, sliding away. "We won't let that happen." Beelzebub keeps his eyes on the wooden bar top as if staring at it will suddenly reveal a solution. "Bee." Michael's hands take his arms and physically turn him around. "I love you. We won't let this destroy our peace agreement or us."

"Promise?"

"That peace agreement is my vow to you. You have my word. I will not break it, and I need yours." Michael smiles at him.

"You would trust the word of a Demon?" Beelzebub snorts. "You're worse off than I thought." He tries to straighten himself out.

"I would trust your word, my love," Michael smiles at him, "We will see this through. We have no other choice but to do so."

Beelzebub looks up into those golden eyes with a firm nod. He slides like water into Michael's arms, and the angel lets out an audible sigh of relief. "How long do you have?" He shouldn't ask because he doesn't want the answer.

"Not long enough, now. Let's talk about something else." He points to the silver tray. "Is that, is that room service?"

Beelzebub shrugs. "Well, it was, kinda ate it all when I thought you weren't coming."

"A binge, huh?" Michael snorts. "I can't leave you alone with food, can I?"

"Nope." Beelzebub shakes his head, "Best get used to it." He smiles, "I am Gluttony." He smirks, "though I have this." He pulls a small wrapped Candy from this pocket and sets it in Michael's palm. "Was from the bedroom, something they call turn-down service, I guess. They leave them on the pillows."

"Pillow candies?" Michael takes it and unwraps it.

"Pillow candies." They laugh together, and Beelzebub can't help how cathartic it feels to be with this angel, this Archangel, this High Commander of Heaven, who loves him so much. Michael pops the candy into his mouth and makes a face but leans in, kissing Beelzebub deeply and pulling him into the bedroom closing the french doors on the bedroom.

V

Raphael

"There's nothingness after destruction. Mathias is not suffering, not anymore." Ariel says, holding Cassiel around the shoulders. "Isn't that Right, Raphael?" Ariel's eyes meet Raphael's. Raphael can feel Ariel's kindness and knows she means well.

"It's true." Raphael smiles sympathetically, "And you don't have to attend the trial Cassiel; only Michael, Gabriel, and I must attend per the statutes." He takes a seat on the other side of the sobbing angel.

"Good-" he sniffles. "I don't want to go. I can't-" he shakes his head, "I feel so responsible! Mathias was one of my people." He sniffles, and sobs. "I felt him go, die, and I-" he shakes his head, "I can't-"

"That's fine, and you're not required to unless Raguel requests your testimony." Ariel says softly, "And if that's the case, we'll work with him and Phanuel to make sure it's not too taxing on you more than it has been."

"I can say no, can't I?" He looks into Raphael's eyes, and his heart breaks for the blonde angel.

Raphael exchanges a look with Ariel before nodding, "Yes, you can say no, but it may not help Heaven's case if you refuse." Raphael runs his fingers through Cassiel's hair and pulls him into a Hug. "We have you, brother."

A knock at the door brings Gabriel. "Ariel, we need you." He closes the door after a brief look at Raphael.

Ariel carefully transitions the lowest of the archangel into Raphael's waiting arms. "I'll be back as quickly as I can."

Cassiel nods and looks at Raphael, "Have you ever felt this? This loss, this amount of pain? I didn't know it would hurt like this..." The door closes as Ariel leaves them.

"No, I have not lost one of my subordinates,"

Raphael answers honestly, "But we must remember Mathias." Raphael nods. "Remember him fondly."

"I do," Cassiel rubs his eyes. "He was funny, always had jokes to tell from the earth."

"Did he?" Raphael smiles softly. "What was your favorite one?"

"Um, it was...when is a door not a door?" He chuckles through his tear-streaked face.

"I don't know. When is a door not a door?" Raphael asks.

"When it's ajar." He chuckles.

Raphael smiles, too, "That's terrible."

"Still funny." Small critters start to cluster at Cassiel's feet.

"Your friends are here." Raphael smiles. "And they look concerned."

Cassiel leans down, lifting one of his rabbits in one hand and two mice in another. "Hello, my dear ones; I'll be okay."

"Yes, you will." Raphael agrees with a bright smile rubbing his hands over Cassiel's arms. "I will keep you updated about the trial."

"That is coming, isn't it?" Cassiel sighs. "What will you wear?"

"Where?" Raphael didn't consider that.

"To the trial. Yeah, my watchers bring me things, shows, books; most people who go to trials wear suits." He says softly and rubs his eyes. "I have some magazines."

"Would that help you ease your mind? To help me find something suitable to wear?" Raphael looks at his robes. "I have worn little else but this attire."

"Come." He shuffles the rabbit into Raphael's arms. "I think we need to work on your earthly information."

"This, coming from an angel who has never been?" Raphael has to smile. "Thank you, brother."

Cassiel turns, leaning down to lift a hedgehog. "Thank you, Raphael, for helping me, and mine find justice."

"It's what brothers do, Cassiel." Raphael smiles and puts his free arm around Cassiel's shoulders while holding the rabbit. "Come on." They stand and go out of the room toward Cassiel's room, a barrage of small animals following along the floor.

When they reach Cassiel's room, Raphael laughs as the little creatures come in and scatter around. "I love what you've done, grass, trees." He turns around. "I like it."

"I wanted something a little different than everyone else." He sniffles and rubs his nose, grabbing up some books on a desk by an oak tree. "Michael has his Television thing, Gabriel, that loud device."

"It's a piano." Raphael smiles, "And he's rather good at it." Raphael smiles, "You should hear the guitar he plays." He smiles, "It's almost like, I'm not sure, but it's lovely."

"It just sounds like noise to me and your room–"

"And what is wrong with my room?"

"It is just filled with books and that bed chair thing."

"It's called a lounge, and I like to read." Raphael smiles. "You know this."

"Yeah, but it's all from God's library," Cassiel says and sniffles again, rubbing his hand over his nose.

Raphael crosses his arms. "And what's wrong with that?"

"I just think you could do with some variety." Cassiel hands him a magazine. "That's a movie star." He points to the man on the cover, a tall black man dressed in a beautiful sequined suit. There is a lovely woman draped on his arm. She is wearing a grey dress with a yellow sash. "See? Aren't they beautiful? Humans are so lovely, so many shapes and colors, all beautiful." Cassiel leans against Raphael and points to the woman. "She's got your hair color."

"I see that." Raphael turns the magazine pages and finds more pictures of the two. "I like the grey." he turns to the next page. The woman's hands are holding a black handbag, and her nails are brightly colored. "What did she do to her fingers?"

"Oh, that's called Nail Paint, I believe."

"Interesting," Raphael says. "It is like art that one wears."

"Exactly." Cassiel turned around in a circle and leaned down, lifting a small rabbit into his arms. "You know what? Take it with you; go down to see Frigg. Show her"

"I shouldn't," Raphael says, folding the book in half and offering it back. "It feels like vanity."

"That's because it is. Go, and take it with you." Cassiel pushes it into his older brother's arms.

"We don't go to Earth," Raphael says.

"No, I don't go to Earth. You've been before." Cassiel shrugs. "Haven't you?"

"That was thousands of years ago," Raphael says

softly. "And I didn't see any people. I was busy with Gabriel."

"Time to see what the new world has, I think." Cassiel smiles at him. "Take it; go see Frigg."

"What about you?" Raphael's hand finds his shoulder.

Cassiel wipes his eyes, "I will be okay." He nods. "I feel much better here; this is my room, after all." Raphael looks up and around. God made their quarters for them. Each room assigned to an angel is designed perfectly around that angel's comfort. They have always felt safest in their own spaces. This space feels like Cassiel, the brave and bold little angel.

Raphael clutches the magazine to his chest. "If you're sure."

Cassiel smiles, "I am. Ariel said she'd stop by later and have tea with me."

Raphael comes forward to hug Cassiel. "If you need me-"

"I know where your room is," Cassiel says softly. "So does Harper." He steps out of the embrace, motioning backward. Raphael assumes Cassiel will send this little critter to fetch him if needed.

"Which one is that again?" Raphael can not keep track of all the critters and their names.

"The mouse." Cassiel turns and points to a mouse sitting on a stump. "Say hello, Harper." Nothing happens; the mouse gets down and runs off. "I'm still working on that."

Raphael smiles, "I'll check in later," He says, Cassiel is already going to his animals. Raphael keeps the book against his chest and exits out the door, He looks back one last time to be sure it's okay to leave Cassiel there before he heads to his room to flip through the magazine's pages.

VI

Beelzebub

"Nergal was trespassing in Heavenly territories, Sire." Lucas, a Duke, and Demonic Lawyer for Hell sit in his chair behind his desk. "That's not easily defensible." Hell's lawyer holds Beelzebub with steely eyes. "The treaties are very clear on that matter, your Highness." He is polite but to the point, which is probably why he's a Duke, and fifth in line for the throne.

"What is Nergal's relationship to the hybrid Quilla? Do we know?" Beelzebub sits across from Lucas' desk and leans back, putting both boots on the desk's edge. Beelzebub notes how Lucas says nothing but doesn't look pleased.

"I believe Nergal is her father." Lucas spins his chair around, turns to another row of files, and pulls open a drawer. "Yes... born to a human woman and Nergal in the late 17th century. She's practically a baby." He smiles, turning the file around, "Nergal did fill out the paperwork and notified us of her birth at the time." He nods, "I must have been the one to file it away; that's my signature." He smacks the paper, setting it on the table.

"Hybrids are not part of our territorial treaties, are they?" Beelzebub asks; he does lift it and scans the document but sets it down.

"No, they are not mentioned. After this, we may need to enact some amendments to handle situations like these. A demon fathered a human hybrid cannot simply walk into Heavenly territories because their offspring are there." He gestures to the sheet. "Heaven agrees with that mentality." He shrugs, "We should start thinking of an amendment to be passed that will satisfy both parties." He shrugs. "Could have the Hybrid leader involved."

"The amendment to our treaties can wait; we

have more important things to discuss. Quilla is Nergal's child. If he went to visit and walked into Heavenly territories, he probably didn't even know; if he did, I doubt he cared. Quilla most certainly didn't have an idea of which territories belong to which sides."

"No, because Hybrids were never part of the territorial negotiations." Lucas nods, "Hence why we need an amendment."

Beelzebub holds up a hand for him to let it go, "We didn't consider this a possibility at all."

"No, we didn't, your Highness, and then the angel Mathias attacked Nergal. Nergal fought back." Lucas stands up, coming around to lean on the desk. "But it doesn't matter; ignorance of territory isn't an excuse." He shrugs, "There's a good chance Heaven will destroy him for this. There's a good chance they have enough evidence for that sort of conviction."

Beelzebub has to consider all this, "What about the self-defense of his daughter? Could we argue that? That perhaps Mathias posed a threat to her?"

"Perhaps, but I would need to speak with her first. Heaven would deny that charge; angels are supposed to be merciful." Lucas rolls his eyes as he grabs another file off his desk, "We still need to find a judge both sides will agree on, and that seems like a fucking nightmare." Lucas shakes his head.

"Heaven won't accept a demon due to bias, and we won't accept an angel for the same reason." Beelzebub takes out his cigarette case and taps it on his hand. "Who is left then?"

"God," Lucas offers, "Or a hybrid." He says, "One that does not have our implicit biases."

"Like who?" Beelzebub pulls a cigarette from the case and puts it between his lips before lighting it. "Who would we get? It's not like Death would do it." It's a mere moment before Beelzebub is on his feet. "I bet he would do it."

"You can't be serious, Sire," Lucas warns.

"Worth a shot." Beelzebub says, turning to the door." We need more information on this Quilla. Does she have other siblings or children? We need to make Heaven have some sympathy if not for Nergal than for them." Lucas seems to get his point and makes a note. "Let me know if you need anything." He says before darting out the door.

His feet hit the ground, and he's down a hallway and running smack dab into Leviathan. Before he can right himself, he's looking up at his taller brother. "Beelzebub."

"Levi." Beelzebub frowns, "I was just headed out to see Death."

"Do you mind if I join you?"

"Not at all, but we better tell Modie she needs to take the throne." Beelzebub says, "Come on, we can do that, and I can grab a lighter."

Leviathan nods at him falling into step as they continue down the hallway. "Of course."

"Do you have anything else planned for the rest of your day?" Beelzebub asks as they fall in step.

"Aye, I must go to Earth to see the Tailor."

"That's not a bad plan. If I send one of my suits with you, could you get her to mend a seam or two? My formal attire hasn't been worn or mended in years."

"Of course." Leviathan smiles. "One would be glad to be of service, and you are most busy."

"I think we're gonna ask Death to be the judge for this trial."

Leviathan stops and raises a brow. "Death?"

"We need an impartial third party lacking bias," Beelzebub says and holds out his arms. "Who better than the ultimate non-bias judge."

Leviathan thins his eyes. "And he will say yes?"

"I don't know, but it doesn't hurt to ask, does it?" Beelzebub beams up at him. "It's the only idea I've got, and I'm open to other suggestions if you have one."

Leviathan puts his hat on his head. "I suppose it would not hurt to ask, but we had best make haste." Leviathan checks his pocket watch before sliding it back into his pocket. "We will need to know if he will not so that we may find an alternative."

"Not sure there is one," Beelzebub sighs, "Let's get this over with."

Beelzebub walks slowly and carefully to the door, adjusting his tie. "How do I look?"

"Royal," Leviathan says as he reaches and holds the door open for Beelzebub. "Go now."

Beelzebub steps through the door and stops to adjust to the strange lighting in this realm. Death's halls are a neutral gray, decorated with black and brown shrouded clothes that cover walls. "Have you been here before, Leviathan? I can't recall."

"Nay, I have never been to the realms of Death."

"Well, today is the day," Beelzebub remembers the route left, right, stop, sign the damn book, and come forward. He notes Michael has been here recently but not since the information of the Death of Mathias.

Leviathan looks over. "A log?"

"He likes to have us sign it." Beelzebub says, "It's a condition of his council." Beelzebub signs it quickly and sets the pen back in the holder. Beelzebub gestures to Leviathan, who comes forward and makes his mark in the book. After he sets the pen back, Beelzebub pulls him along. "This way."

He turns down another hallway towards large doors that open before they near them. The shroud of Death stands up out of his seat. "Children, excuse us." Two beings, one angel and one demon turn to bow at Death and then exit to either side of the room.

"Who are your subordinates?" Leviathan asks. "A demon and an angel?"

The shroud motions to Beelzebub. "They sort the souls for each realm." He nods. "They belong to him and are effectively his heralds; it was an agreement with God before we were made that two would be given to him to serve." Beelzebub sighs. "The fewer of us who know that, brother, the better."

Leviathan nods, "I shall keep thine secret." He bows his head.

Death turns to Beelzebub, "Speak your desires."

"An angel has been killed by one of our people," Beelzebub says softly.

"Mathias, yes," he murmurs, looking at a book that floats in front of him. "Yes, his destruction is known."

"We need a third party to oversee the trial," Beelzebub says calmly. "We have come to implore your aid."

"Why do you wish this to be me?"

Leviathan steps past where Beelzebub stands. "Oh powerful Death, thine opinion is well respected, and there are well known for thine ability not to take sides. Thee who are the true weigher of the soul."

Death looks at Beelzebub, "What he said." Beelzebub pulls a cigarette out but doesn't light it. "We need an unbiased third party."

"Has Heaven agreed?" Death asks softly.

"I'm sure they will." Beelzebub nods. "I know you can communicate with Micahel."

"I will consider your proposal. You will have my answer in one Earth hour." Death vanishes, and the two beings come back out from their doors and return to their work, ignoring the demons in the middle of the hall.

"Come on, Levi, that's the best we can do for now."

Leviathan nods, "Let us hope he decides in our great favor."

Beelzebub lights the cigarette hanging from his lips with a nod. "Let's get back, brother; we have much to prepare for."

"Aye." Leviathan nods. "I need to leave for the tailors; get me the suit you wish altered."

"I'll ensure Hauster gets it to you before you depart." Beelzebub smacks his arm gently.

VII

Raphael

Raphael pushes open the door to enter a shop in a tiny town in the middle of rural Canada. The establishment is the tailor's shop, it is one of the few places Raphael ever goes to on earth. Raphael sees little need for such personal items, but with the trial approaching, a suit sounds like it's something he needs to get made. He has an idea and a small picture he's clipped from the magazine Cassiel gave him, a white suit, a Gold tie, and a gold pocket square. Cassie had said it looked brilliant. Raphael hopes it does because he wants it in grey, similar to the suits like Micahel wears.

The immortal Hybrid known as Frigg runs the establishment and has for many years. She is the most extraordinary seamstress on the earth. Always at work with new designs. That's where Raphael finds her, fast at work, pressing a pin into the collar of a customer who stands before three mirrors. "General Raphael." She greets him when he walks into the door. "It's been a long time. How wonderful to see you again!" The customer who is with her is standing very. Still, there are pins along a leather collar. Most of the suit the man wears appears to be leather, hide, or animal. "I'll be just a moment."

"By all means, of course." He beams brightly and steps aside to wait. He looks down at the clipping in his hand of a suit, with gold accents and a bright golden tie. The woman next to the man in the photo looks fetching too, with a golden dress and beautifully painted nails.

"A General of Heaven is here?" the man who is before the mirrors asks Frigg and turns to look him up and down. Raphael turns the clipping to himself, hiding it.

"Yes, Sire." Frigg smiles, standing to make

the introduction. "General Raphael, Archangel of Health and Healing."

The man turns and pauses as Raphael locks onto his red eyes and says nothing. This person isn't a man. This person is a demon. "General Raphael," Frigg stands, "this is his Royal Highness Prince Leviathan, of Hell, Prince of the ocean depths, patron of envy."

Leviathan bows his head politely. "General, it is a pleasure to meet you, though I wish it were under different circumstances." Raphael isn't sure why the demon is being kind. It must be the treaties that keep him behaving. Frigg's shop is a neutral territory, after all.

"Highness," Raphael responds curtly, unsure of what to say to that.

Leviathan turns his eyes to the seamstress. "One moment, Sir." Frigg goes behind a curtain. "I'll fetch your hat."

"I see we came to the same conclusions." The Prince says and relaxes his stance. "That we required a tailor."

"It appears we did. Frigg is the best tailor in any realm." Raphael smiles. It is a truth, no doubt about it. "No one is better in Heaven or on Earth."

"Aye, tis true, nor in Hell. On that, we can agree." Leviathan smiles. "This shall be interesting, this trial." He says kindly. "Will it not?"

"We probably should not speak to each other about the trial as it draws near," Raphael says and folds his hands before himself. He doesn't want to speak to a demon about it. Raphael hides the clippings in his palm but keeps his polite smile. He cannot help but fall apart as the demon looks at him with a skeptical glance.

Leviathan shrugs, red eyes glowing brighter, and now Raphael can see they look like rubies. "We shall be there merely to bear witness as figureheads of our realms. Aye, mere trinkets on a shelf." He waves a hand; his voice is gentle yet firm. "Lucas will defend our confined demon. Your angelic lawyers will prosecute." he shrugs. "A judge will be found to ...decide his fate." He shrugs. "Nay. Us speaking, having opinions on the subject, well, tis a moot point. Our stance on the issue is for naught." Raphael marvels again at how he holds himself. This Prince is intelligent and dignified.

"I didn't see why I needed to go anyway," Raphael says with a smile. Completely understanding where this demon is coming from, he didn't want to go, Michael insisted.

"You see," Leviathan smiles, "My Lord, I completely agree."

"Michael said it was for" Raphael can't help but roll his golden eyes.

"Presentation," Leviathan says at the same time Raphael does.

"That's precisely it, yes." Raphael shakes his head. "Just what we need more pageantry." They laugh together. That part feels nice.

"Indeed, Beelzebub said much the same to my arguments," Leviathan says, looking Raphael up and down before turning to notice Frigg, who has returned with a black leather hat with a long red feather. "Ah, my hat, many thanks." He takes it when offered and puts it upon his head. "Is there more you need from me, Madam Frigg?"

"No, sire, leave your suit, and you're free to go. I'll have it hand-delivered to Hell. Along with Prince Beelzebub's suit." She beams at him.

With a wave of his hand and Leviathan's suit is draped on a mannequin, and he is wearing something that looks less formal. Leather jacket and trousers. Dark browns and blacks and his cuffs adorned by golden buttons on the cuffs and the center of the coat. He makes a motion to his hat. "I can take my hat with me, yes?"

"Yes, your Highness, of course." Frigg nods. "All feathers replaced."

Leviathan smiles and turns to Raphael, the demon being slightly taller. "I will see you on the morrow, General Raphael?"

"Yes, Prince Leviathan, you will."

"Then good day to thee, General." he turns, tipping his hat to Frigg. "Madam tailor." Before grabbing the handle of the door, "Please complete the alterations. Beelzebub and I will need them by tomorrow."

"As I said, you will have them tonight, your Highness." She beams at him.

With a final nod at Raphael, the demon slips out the door. "Is he always like that?"

Frigg laughs, "There's a reason the term 'Charming Devil' exists, and I'm pretty sure-" she wiggles her scissors at the door. "It's because of him."

Raphael smiles and walks forward, handing her the small clipping. "Is this something you might be able to make for me?" He wavers between the two but settles on the masculine form, "I want it grey, but can the tie match her dress?"

She smiles. "I have just the thing, one moment." She smiles. "And we'll get you all sorted out." Raphael smiles as Frigg takes his hand. "Your nails..." He notes their beautiful red color. "How do you get them to have color?"

"I paint them." She smiles, "would you like to have a nail enamel to match? I can show you how. It's not hard."

Raphael beams, "Yes." He smiles. "Please?" Maybe Cassie was right, and he needed a change. "And these." he touches her bracelets.

"I'll get some things together; hop up on the stand for me. You're going to look stunning. I'll make sure of it." Frigga exits the room. Raphael steps up and notes a small red feather from the demon's cap. He leans down and picks it up off the ground, and puts it in his pocket. He doesn't know why he did, but he pats that pocket protectively.

VIII

Beelzebub

Beelzebub and Lucas arrive in the Empty Realm. The angels have done a marvelous job; there are risers and seats everywhere—tables out front for the prosecution and defense, a large center seat for Death.

Beelzebub has to take a moment to adjust the collar on his suit. The suit alterations are exceptional, with silver-toned accents that match his cigarette case. It was delivered the night before, and he appreciates the few extra added details the Frigg decided upon on her own.

"This is bound to be fun," Lucas says sarcastically, holding his briefcase. "I still can't believe you got Death to be the judge. Masterful work, your Highness."

"Don't worry about it," Beelzebub says softly and nudges Lucas' arm. "There's Nergal." They start forward. There is a holy cage of sorts; Nergal is kneeling inside. Hands to either side, meditating. Moss is growing along the brown collar of his jacket. It's also growing on the floor and the cage. "What is that?"

"Nergal is one of the elementals, Highness, they can stop a lot of his demonic power with the warding, but elements will still come to him; the moss is growing toward him, not out from him. It's seeking him out."

"Which is why we aren't stopping it." Solas, Heaven's head of security, looks between them. "I am Solas, a representative of Heaven. Only his council may speak with him."

"That's fine." Beelzebub motions Lucas along to speak to Nergal. "Thank you. Lucas, I'll leave you to your client."

Lucas walks off, and Beelzebub turns away. "Where are the seats for the royal family?"

"Up at the top of the stands, sir." Sola's points. "Hell to the Left, Heaven to the right."

Beelzebub looks up, sees the seats, and smiles. While they are not close, he and Michael are seated parallel. He closes his eyes, briefly allowing the warm sun to lay on his face and enjoy the moment. He does like earth. It has things Hell doesn't. Sun and warm breezes are his favorite. The Empty Realm exists on earth, but humans will never find it. It's been a long time since Beelzebub was outside.

A throat clears, and Beelzebub opens his eye and turns to the Angel before him. "Hello, I am Raguel." The taller dark haired Angel walks forward.

"Beelzebub, Crown Prince of Hell." Beelzebub holds out his hand, but the Angel shakes his head, clearly disinterested in the handshake.

"We hope you understand the gravity of such a conviction."

Beelzebub lowers his hand and nods, "I do, and so does Nergal." He looks around. Many people are already in the stands, and seats fill up with angels and demons to witness the trial.

"This is my brother Phanuel," Raguel says, pointing behind him.

"Twins?"

"No, I was created first. Phanuel came just after."

Phanuel comes forward and extends a hand that Beelzebub shakes. "You can call me Han." He beams.

"That's enough, Phanuel." Phanuel backs away from Beelzebub at his brother's stern warning.

Beelzebub looks at the taller Angel. "Is the Hybrid here and her child?"

"Yes, Quilla, and her son." Raguel nods, "Your counselor will be able to speak with her."

"Good," Beelzebub nods. "All seems well in hand. Thank you so much for being so cooperative."

"And Heaven thanks you for your cooperation as well," Phanuel adds, but his brother's stern look silences Phanuel.

"For now, your Highness, you may take your seat. There's a throne for you just there." Raguel turns, pointing at the seats Solas had told him about before. Raguel turns his head to glare at his brother again, an act that causes the younger Angel to go silent. Beelzebub sighs; that's not good.

"A throne, you say?" Beelzebub smirks. "Pulled out all the stops, did we?"

"You would have to ask the High Commander." Raguel looks away.

"Will he be in attendance?" Beelzebub asks Raguel.

"Of course, he will." Raguel turns. "Come, brother, we must discuss these outbursts." the more petite Angel goes with him but glances back at Beelzebub briefly.

Beelzebub walks up the center of the room's stairs to the seats in the higher part of the styled auditorium seats. Thrones, not so much, just seating; Beelzebub and Michael look to be seated on the highest level to oversee the trial.

"I hope they are to your liking." a soft voice says.

Beelzebub turns and sees the Angel speaking to him. "I am Prince Beelzebub."

"Ariel." She smiles at him. "Michael, Raphael, and Gabriel will be along shortly." She says, turning to their seats to lay out small notebooks and pens.

"Will you be joining us?" Beelzebub asks.

The golden-eyed Angel with dark hair and dark skin shakes her head. "I leave things like this to others with far more interest for justice." She beams at him. "Have a good day, Your Highness." She does bow, which catches him off guard before she turns and leaves him. No angel has shown such respect to him before, save for Micahel.

"Brother." Leviathan's voice catches Beelzebub's attention. "This had best be quick." He is pulling at his coat's sleeves and looking at the seats.

"Do you have somewhere to be?" Beelzebub chuckles and smiles as Asmodeus, Leviathan's twin, comes to his side. "Hello, dear sister." he leans in, kissing her on the cheek before stepping back to look at Leviathan.

"Nay, but I would rather not be here; you must understand." he looks around. "If the angels bring Holy water, I cannot command it; you know this. My ability to protect us from it will be for naught."

"I do understand. We have treaties in place for a reason, Leviathan. Micahel doesn't want war with Hell," Beelzebub motions to the seats. "Worry not."

"Thine trust in Michael does not grant peace

for my mind." Leviathan scowls. "For all we know, this could simply be a trap." He looks scared.

"Well, good thing I'm in charge. Find your seat, brother." Beelzebub smiles.

"Well, they didn't have to stand for such a ceremony on our accounts, but I won't complain." Asmodeus takes her brother's arm. "Come sit before you make a worse scene."

"Aye, fair sister." He goes with his sister, and they sit in their chairs. Asmodeus takes Leviathan's hand and smiles at Beelzebub.

Beelzebub lingers in the doorway as if willing Michael to appear. When he doesn't, Beelzebub takes his seat.

The next being passing through the doorway is a beautiful specimen of an Angel. One Beelzebub does not recall meeting. The Angel must be Gabriel or Raphael; he isn't exactly sure. Beelzebub notes how Leviathan sits forward in his seat. The Angel wears a soft grey suit with gold accents, flowers on his lapel, and up in his long red hair.

"One of their Generals?" Asmodeus asks. "Who is that Beelzebub?"

Leviathan speaks before he can answer. "General Raphael of Health and Healing," Leviathan says.

"You shouldn't desire something that isn't for you." Asmodeus pulls out her journal and writes down a few notes. "Brother, that's simply a terrible idea."

"Wanting has never hurt anyone," Leviathan argues to her. Beelzebub just smiles. "Sometimes it's the having that does not live to the expectations of the wants."

"Is that so?" Beelzebub smiles brightly at him.

"This." He answers softly and leans back in his chair, meeting Beelzebub's smirk before he looks away.

"What Angel hurt you?" Asmodeus doesn't look up as she asks.

"Not an angel," Leviathan sighs, "and they were no one." It wasn't an Angel who hurt him, it was a human, and Beelzebub remembers the depths of Leviathan's pain. People can salvage some relationships, and others cannot.

At that moment, Michael walks through the door and meets his eyes. Beelzebub swallows hard, turning away to look elsewhere. He catches Asmodeous looking back at him, but she says nothing, and for that, he is thankful. Being a brother to

Asmodeus, who can see your every desire, even if vaguely, is not fun sometimes.

IX

Michael

Gabriel is decidedly late, and Micahel sighs, motioning him up to where he and Raphael are already waiting for him. Gabriel sees his hand and comes their way, trotting up the stairs to their seats, giving the demons a sidelong glance before focusing on Michael. "There you are." Michael sighs, "Where were you?"

"Sorry, Metatron sent a note, and I had to get it to the facilitator."

"Is he alright?" Michael asks softly.

"Fine, just running out of his fruit." Gabriel shrugs. "Facilities will run to the garden and get him more," Gabriel says softly. "Was the last thing I needed to do. I didn't know how long we'd be."

"And Ariel is holding office?"

"Yes, Ariel is handing some of the Heavenly duties to Cassiel, and if they need us, they'll send someone down to grab us," Gabriel says. "If needed, I can step away and go handle it. You need to be here."

Michael can't argue that. He glances at Beelzebub, one leg hooked over the other smoking, as he looks at Michael and winks. Michael turns his head away and looks at Raphael. "We should take our seats; Death will be here soon–"

"PLEASE BE SEATED!" An unfamiliar voice booms over the room. The room is a sudden scurry of order and then silence. "All rise for the honorable and immeasurable Death." The angel announcer steps backward, and a shadowy phantom appears at the top of the main chair. Michael has seen Death before and spoken to him a few times, but Death is rarely ever seen, and even rarer still that he is outside of his domain.

Death is tall, taller than everything around him, a towering shroud. Long spindly fingers exit from the veil, pointing at Raguel below. "Proceed." The voice is harmonic and hollow, an echo in a room where no echo should exist. He points to the table on the left.

An angel at one of the tables stands. "I am Raguel, Archangel of Justice." He says, kindly rounding the table. "I am Heaven's chosen representative, and I work with my fellow Archangel Phanuel, an angel of Judgement," a gesture behind him to the other angel at the table, "to seek out Justice and ensure that we get to the bottom of the most important facet of it."

"That being?" Death's shroud tilts to the left.

"The truth, your honor." He nods. "The truth of what happened to our brother Mathais a Watcher and Angel of Heaven."

"Hell?" Death's shrouded hand moves to the right.

Michael has never seen Hell's attorney. The shorter demon stands politely and bows his head. "I am the Duke Lucas of the Legion of his Highness, Crown Prince Beelzebub, and I am here to defend my brother Nergal from destruction."

"Brother?" Death drones, "Explain."

"Yes, your Honor, we are of the same Legion, under Beelzebub." He says softly. "And I intend to do my best to make sure we remain brothers." he lifts his arm and rolls up his sleeve, the fly mark on his arm evident. "Nergal bears the same mark."

There are murmurs in the crowd, demons, and angels.

"Heaven, you may proceed." Death leans back, almost appearing to sit down. Lucas turns back to his table and sits opening folders as Raguel stands up, coming around to address the court.

Raguel turns to Lucas, and the two shake hands before he turns to the amassed crowd. "A murder has been committed. A killing, on sacred, Holy ground-" Michael sighs and sits back. All he can do is watch.

There's a breathy sound beside him. Turning, he can see Beelzebub tap his cigarette over the ashtray on his armrest, seeming to listen. Beelzebub meets his eyes and winks again, damn him. Michael turns his attention back to the floor.

X

Beelzebub

The angel across the buffet table hands Beelzebub a warm coffee. He smiles looking down; she also offers him a donut on a napkin with a note seeming to peer through the edges. Beelzebub thanked her before turning to a table in the far corner of the room. Once alone pulls the paper free and smiles.

'This is torture' - M.

Beelzebub laughs before glancing over at him across the room, shaking his head. Their eyes meet, and Beelzebub nods at him. Michael, who is seemingly ignoring everything Gabriel is chatting with him about, just smiles. Message confirmed. The trial is indeed torture for Beelzebub. he looks back down at his coffee and sighs quietly before starting to eat the donut.

"Brother-" Leviathan sits down quickly into a seat beside him. Beelzebub palms the small note and stuffs it in his pocket. "Father sent word via Hastur. He would like an update. I sent a message that there isn't much to report on yet, but that should there be a change in circumstances, I will send work back as soon as possible."

"Anything else?"

"Father wished to know if he was needed here with us." Leviathan shrugs and looks past Beelzebub briefly, toward the Angels in the corner at their table. "I told him not right now." He says kindly and looks at a lesser demon, one of his legionnaires, and snaps a finger. Soon, fresh coffee appears before Leviathan with a small dish of sugar. "Thank you." he dismisses the demon away.

"We can handle this Leviathan," Beelzebub says softly.

"I'd like to think that we could, dear brother, but this will meet its end," he explains, dropping sugar cubes in his coffee. "One way or the other."

Beelzebub turns his head now, red eyes narrow. "Levi." The prince before him meets his eyes and says nothing. "We can handle this."

Leviathan looks behind him, and Beelzebub knows he's afraid of those angels; they all are. To see people who have something that they do not deserve, something they can never get back. "I hope so."

"Good." Beelzebub leans back. "Where is your sister?"

"Talking to Lucas." Leviathan leans back in his seat. "To find what he doth think of the whole matter, this Raguel is a nightmare."

"He is an angel, and his word is the law; it's what he does." Beelzebub explains, "His brother is Judgement, and he Justice-"

"And neither tis unbiased."

"This is how Justice will work. We covered Justice all of those years ago when we, Michael and I, made territorial alliances. We have just never had to use this sort of Justice system, but Nergal destroyed an Angel, and we must be accommodating."

Leviathan leans down on the table. "A century

ago, Nergal would have praised him, nay, hailed a hero!"

"He was protecting his daughter and grandchild," Beelzebub says softly. "I could no sooner blame him knowing well what our father would do to protect us." He keeps his voice low and quiet between the two of them.

Leviathan gestures widely. "Is that why our father is concerned with whether he should be here?"

"Perhaps." Beelzebub shrugs, "But I don't claim to speak on behalf of our father's wishes. I never have. I know better."

Leviathan leans back in his seat. An angel appears in the recreation room doorway and clears her throat. "The court will return to session in ten minutes." Angels and demons in the room start to stand to make their way back to the courtroom.

"That's us," Beelzebub says and drinks down the rest of the coffee in a shot, grabbing the remaining piece of donut. "Let's hope Asmodeus isn't far."

Leviathan walks directly behind him to his left. Asmodeus is not around, and Beelzebub wonders, fondly, if she even left her seat.

That is where they find their sister lounging in her seat with a book, reading. "Sister." Beelzebub stalls between their chairs. Leviathan drops into his seat as Beelzebub pulls out his silver engraved cigarette case. He taps the case on his palm before pulling out one of the slim cigarettes.

"You aren't going to continue to smoke here, are you?" She scolds even as she pulls out a lighter.

"Demonic proclivities." Beelzebub smiles in argument but allows her to light the cigarette in his hands. "I'm a prince." He puffs at it with the flame and hmms in pleasure.

"Is that your excuse?" She chuckles.

"Yes," Beelzebub smiles. "Thank you." He takes a draw and blows the smoke out his nose, careful to look around the room. He sees Michael sitting down in his seat behind Gabriel and Raphael. Beelzebub nods to his siblings and steps up to his throne behind them. He sits back and taps his cigarette in the ashtray provided, hooking one knee over the other.

XI

Michael

The trial has gone on for hours now. Both sides give testimony, show off their maps, and discuss treaties and lines. How things may or may not be related to what happened. Heaven talks at length about their Fallen Angel Mathias, how holy he was, noble. They speak of his record, his decorations, and his work. It's a neat little package.

Near the end of the day, the Hybrid woman, Quilla, has been called to the stand where she sits holding her infant child. It's been a long day, and it's evident on her face how tired she is. It's not just the trial, but it's tending to her minor child, with her seated in her lap facing her. She has a large bag at her side, and she's struggling to keep her focus on the angel who questions her.

"Can you state your name for the record?" Raguel asks.

"My name is Quilla." She says, bouncing the baby on her lap gently. "Shhh, it's okay." Michael smiles at her.

"And who are your parents?" Raguel leans back on his table.

"My mother was a human. I don't remember her name, I- It's been a long time since I can't remember her, not well anyway." She looks to the cage, where Nergal simply meets her eyes. She shifts the baby from her lap to her shoulder, "My father is the Demon known as Nergal, I have known him my entire life, and he has always been part of my life." She points to the cage.

"And do you possess any powers?" Raguel shrugs. "Magic of any kind, tricks?"

"No, Sir. To my knowledge, no Hybrids have powers." The child in her lap starts to fuss a bit, and she bounces the baby on her knee, attention split between the child and the questions. "Shhhh, it's okay."

"None?"

"No." Her eyes snap up to meet Raguels. "I'm just an immortal like all other hybrid species."

Raguel seems pleased by the answer, nodding and circling back. "On the day in question, what were you doing?" Raguel asks. "What were your Earthly plans?" Michael sighs profoundly and tries to focus, but the baby in her arms is nearly crying out.

"Dinner with my father." She says, looking back at the cage. Michael feels a twinge of something about the look they share. It's clear to him that she loves her father. She bounces the child a bit more, transitioning it again to the other shoulder.

"Special occasion?" Raguel gestures widely. His questions are tame enough, but Michael makes a note to talk to him about his tone.

"Yes, my son's birthday." She says. "He'd turned one." The child begins to fuss more, and Michael frowns. It is a distraction. Quilla looks up, "I'm sorry; I'll try to keep him quiet."

Raguel nods, "The child is not an issue." He says calmly. "We just need you to answer the questions." Michael sighs; the child is a great distraction to those in the auditorium.

The crowd around him gasps. When Michael looks over, Beelzebub snuffs out his cigarette and makes his way down to the floor and Quilla.

"Prince Beelzebub, you will not interfere." The shroud of Death stands speaking in a booming voice. "You may not approach the bench."

"I'm not interfering with the proceedings, your honor." Beelzebub stops and motions to the child. "I am removing a distraction so that she may answer the court fully; as the child is a quarter demon, I will take that responsibility on. She has a right to give a fair testimony, and she can not do that and juggle the child at the same time." He says, "We hope Heaven would not deny her the right to speak her truth."

Michael smiles as Raguel turns to meet his eyes. Micahel nods with a small gesture. Raguel turns to Death, "Your Honor, it would be easier to question if the child could be managed away from the stand."

"Very well, Prince Beelzebub; please take the child and return to your seat." Death leans back. "Heaven, you may finish your questions."

Beelzebub gently takes the child before turning and returning to his seat. Michael watches as Beelzebub rocks the child in his arms, making soothing sounds. Micahel can smell vanilla in the air, odd.

"This is ridiculous." Gabriel leans back to meet his eyes. "That is a disruption of the court." He gestures, "How does this not go in their favor."

Michael leans down to meet Gabriel's ear. "The child screaming is more a disruption, brother; we need Raguel and Phanuel to have the best chance at winning this, do we not? Getting her clear and concise answers will best facilitate that." He keeps his voice a whisper. "Trust me; we are the more merciful party by allowing it."

"Yes," Gabriel accepts this answer, thankfully. "Yes, of course, brother."

"Well, let the demons care for the child," Raphael smirks and turns his head back.

Michael's eyes pitch forward as Raguel continues to speak to her. "So you were having dinner to celebrate your son's birthday." Raguel nods. "And you invited your father." Raguel gestures, "That all seems like a normal family gathering. My next question is, how old are you, hybrid?"

"Objection!" Lucas stands, Death and the room remain quiet when spindled fingers point at Lucas, and he continues. "Council will refer to the witness by her name, Quilla."

Raguel holds up his hands before Death can speak, already accepting the challenge, "I will re-state my question. Quilla, how old are you?"

"I am seven hundred and forty-two years of age." She looks up at Beelzebub, who keeps the child occupied. It suits him to hold the child. Michael can only smile when he looks at the child, whose red eyes and unruly dark hair remind him of the prisoner below.

"And this is your first child?" Raguel points up to where Beelzebub sits.

"Um, my third." She says softly.

"And the others?" Raguel turns around. "Where are they?"

"With only Quarter demonic blood, they are human, and they died many years ago." She snif-fles. "Nelle and Gallant." She nods "both gone, one in 1467 and the other in 1765."

"You outlived them?"

"I outlive all humans, but my children never really lived." She shrugs and reaches up to wipe her eyes. Michael sees Nergal standing at the edge of his cage, looking only at his daughter. "The only gift I have is my immortality, but a curse in that I outlive my children. The worst part is they don't even live very long in the first place."

Raguel does lower his voice a moment, "The children died young?"

"As infants, yes to sickness." she reaches up, wiping her eyes.

Michael turns to look at the child. Whom Beelzebub is charming with what looks like a silver ring. The child's hands are around the circle, looking up with red eyes passed down from his grandfather Nergal to his mother and then to him.

"What is this child's name?" Raguel points up to Beelzebub.

"Issac Nergal, after his grandfather," she says softly.

"You know he's a demon-" Raguel says.

"Objection!" Lucas stands, "Irrelevant. Of course, she knows her father is a demon."

"Sustained." Death says, "Keep it to the topic at hand, Raguel."

"Of course," Raguel gives Lucas an unflattering glance as Michael leans back in his chair, unable to move. "Did you see the fight between your father, Nergal, and the Watcher angel, Mathias?"

"Yes, some of it." She says with a nod. "We were eating dinner. The angel burst through the door."

"He came after your Father?"

"Yes." She nods

"Do you know why?"

Quilla looks at Michael directly and shrugs before her eyes turn back to Raguel. "No, I don't." She shrugs. "We were having dinner. Father was holding Isaac-" A gesture to Beelzebub, who holds the child who is now sleeping soundly against the prince's chest.

"Nergal was in Angelic territories." Raguel informs her. "Did you know that?" She shakes her head at him. "He was trespassing. He was not where he should have been."

"But I am his daughter." She argues.

"He was in our territories. Your father, per our treaties, should have known where the boundaries were," Raguel says, "How did your father kill the angel that attacked him?" The questions swing back to the fight.

"With a long-bladed weapon." She says softly. "His weapon."

"Do you know what the name of that weapon is?" Raguel turns to the evidence table.

"A scimitar, it's a type of sword." She says softly, hands gesturing a shape.

Raguel lifts the weapon. It's got a small tag on it and is in a clear bag. "This one?"

"Yes." She nods. "That's my father's weapon or at least one that looks like it. There's a sapphire in the handle. It reminds him of me, he tells me." She looks at her father in the cage and smiles at him brightly.

"What do you know about the weapons angels and demons carry?" Raguel asks.

"I know that each of you has one, a weapon and that most are unique extensions of your bodies."

Raguel smiles, a pleasing look across his face. "That's right, and what weapon did the angel possess?"

"It looked like an ax of some kind, short and blunt." She shrugs. "Like a hatchet?"

Raguel nods, lifting another bag. "Like this one." The weapon in the pack is broken into many pieces.

"Yes."

Michael leans forward in his seat; he glances at Beelzebub, who is watching just as intently as he is. The child is asleep in his arms, "What was the killing blow?" Raguel's question draws his eyes back to the floor.

"I didn't see it."

Raguel frowns and shakes his head, "Forgive me, you said you saw the battle?"

"I said I saw some of it, and father did tell me to turn my head away at one point."

"At what point did that happen?" He folds his arms over his broad chest.

"At the end." She purses her lips, "I held Isacc tightly and turned us away, shielding our eyes."

"Then what did you hear?"

She looks at the angelic lawyer and shakes her head, "There was a bright light, then there was nothing."

Raguel nods, "I have no further questions, your honor."

Death nods, "Hell, you have the floor."

Michael watches Raguel sit down, and Lucas stands up to button the top button of his jacket. He walks over to the woman on the stand and smiles. "My name is Lucas Quilla. It's nice to meet you." he nods. "How long did you live at the location where your home is?" He pulls out a map to show Death the marker over the boundary and then indicates the angels on their side.

Michael notes how she looks down. "A very long time, four, five hundred years?"

"Wouldn't someone notice a woman who does not age?"

"I change my name every 60 to 80 years or so...move away from time to time, pass the house back to myself." She nods. "We've learned how to hold onto a property with human rules."

"Who do you speak of when you use the term 'we'?"

"Oh, hybrids, we have lots of rules." She gestures, "Tricks, things we can do. It is how immortals survive."

"Of course," Lucas nods. "So, is the birthday meal a tradition? With your father? Did he come to the birthdays of..." He looks at his notes. "Nelle and Gallant?"

"Yes, my father was at every birthday, every milestone, everything he could be at, burials too."

"So he's been involved in your life the entire time."

"Since my mother died when I was young." She

nods, "He has always been in contact. He never leaves me high and dry and is always there when I need him. He's always there for my kids for as long as they are around."

"But your kids never had kids."

"Objection." Raguel stands for "Relevance?"

Death looks at Lucas. "Your honor, I'm trying to establish that this was ordinary. That Nergal's actions were repetitive, and you could count on them to happen, and if the treaties have been in place for as long as they have, perhaps Heaven was not paying close enough attention, or they didn't care until now. I'm trying to establish the motive for him being where he was. Establishing his extended family is a way to ascertain that."

"Which we did; it was the birthday party," Raguel argues.

"Correct. Quilla states her father is there for every milestone yes? That means he's been coming here for years, with no intervention from Heaven. I need to establish Heaven's non-activity in the years between the signing of the treaties and now," Lucas says, turning to Death. "Your honor, we need to know what happened and what motivated it, and the best way to get through to those answers is this line of questioning. Heaven wants to prove wrongdoing, but I intend to prove otherwise."

Death considers and nods, "Overruled."

Lucas bows to Death. "Your children never had children. Your lines end with your children?"

"All Hybrids can have kids, but most of our kids are sterile." There is collective chatter throughout the room, and Death holds up his hand to silence the room. "And mine died so young; they never had the chance to have their own families."

"So meeting his grandchildren is the farthest into the family one of our kind, demon or angel could get?"

"That's correct." She looks up at Beelzebub, who nods at her holding the baby against his chest. Michael turns his head to look at Beelzebub and takes in the image of the Demon. The child is sleeping against Beelzebub's chest, the silver ring locked tightly in a grip. There is a vibration in the air, and the vanilla smell is lingering.

"So, the question I have is this, now follow me here-" Lucas looks at Raguel and then at Death. "If Nergal's been visiting his daughter, beyond those boundaries, for hundreds of years. I have to ask myself why an Angel attacked him. Why now? What changed?"

"Objection!" Raguel stands up. "This was not an attack from Heaven."

Lucas looks right at Death, "My Lord, per her testimony, Mathias kicked in her door and came after Nergal. That is the absolute definition of an attack." Lucas doesn't look at Raguel at all.

"Overruled." Death says, "Get to the point, council."

Lucas takes two steps toward the bench but speaks loudly enough for the whole chamber to hear him. "I ask the court to consider that something else was going on between Nergal and the angel Mathias." the surrounding room breaks into whispers and chatter, "I would like to see what caused something seemingly fine for hundreds of years to go sour suddenly. Hell requests a week of Discovery, and I would like to see the watcher records regarding sightings of demons in this territory only."

Gabriel looks back at Michael and frowns. Michael holds up a hand for him to wait. "Just listen, Gabriel."

Death rises and looks around the room. "I will afford two days of Discovery. Heaven will give Hell's councilor access to this territory's last four hundred years of record. Hell will give Heaven all its records of Nergal and his children; get your notes in order. Two days. This session is adjourned." Death vanishes.

Michael and the entire room stand slowly and quietly from their seats. Beelzebub included the sleeping baby in his arms. Raguel folds his folder and looks at his brother, but Michael notes how smug the Demon Lucas looks.

Michael turns his head to Beelzebub as the room starts to disperse. "It suits you."

Gabriel frowns at him. "Don't compliment them, Michael."

Michael shoves his hands in his pockets. "We'll see you in two days, Prince Beelzebub." Michael inclines his head. It's not a bow but a gesture.

"You as well, High Commander." Beelzebub turns now to Quilla, who comes to take the child from his grasp.

"Thank you, your highness." She bows her head.

Beelzebub lays a hand on her head, bestowing countenance as a priest would. Michael finds it fascinating. "They do care for their own. It is interesting to see it first hand." Raphael is at his side in a heartbeat.

The two angels watch as the royal family each takes turns putting a hand on the child. "All they have is one another, Raphael, since they are no longer of Heaven. All they have is what they are left with."

"And that is their family?"

"I think so." Michael nods. "Ours is a family too, isn't it, brother?"

"Yes." Raphael smiles and steps past Micahel. Michael watches Raphael step up to one of the Demonic Princes. Based on what he knows, this must be Leviathan.

"What is he doing?" Gabriel asks as he steps into Raphael's vacated place. "He shouldn't talk to them."

"I haven't the slightest." Michael folds his arms to watch. "But Raphael was never one to take too many risks."

Raphael reaches into his pocket and pulls out a red feather, saying nothing and handing it to the prince before walking down the stairs and away. "Strange." Gabriel frowns.

"Indeed, but no harm in returning a feather," Michael says and turns to him. "Let's get back to Heaven; we have two days to get things in order before we're right back here."

"Agreed." Gabriel gestures for Michel to go down the stairs first. He chances one more glance at Beelzebub and then heads down the stairs toward the exit.

XII

Leviathan

Hell is at least quiet when they return. "You spoke to one of the angels today," Asmodeus says as they walk back down the main hallway. "What was his name, Gabriel?" She waves a hand, "I can't tell them apart."

"No, that was General Raphael." He shakes his head, "And he did not speaketh to me." He says, "Simply coming to return a feather that had fallen from my cap." He reaches into his pocket and pulls out a red feather to show his sister before pocketing it again.

"Uh-huh." Asmodeus smiles. "You like him."

"Perhaps," He shrugs, "But I dare not venture into Heavenly bodies again; tis not a desire of mine to be hurt. I shall leave that sort of behavior to our dear brother."

"Oh, what was her name? The last one, the human."

"I dare not say," Leviathan says softly.

"I can just pull it from your mind." his sister teases.

"Thou wouldst not." He looks at her. "One must insist on one's autonomy. I love thee, indeed, as your love for me is known. You would not violate my mind for thine own gain, and I know thee too well for that."

"Very well." She smiles. "But answer me this." They stop in the hallway, "How long has it been?"

"Since my heart was entwined thus?" Leviathan nods, "Four hundred years, but that does not mean I wish to entwine myself again, and least to a general of Heaven." He tries to sound reasonable because, at this point, the chances of him and a General of Heaven falling in love are completely and utterly ridiculous. "I'm not a simpleton sister."

Asmodeus beams, "You're right. That's ridiculous."

"Indeed, a folly. I love thee." He gently kisses her cheek before he walks past her, "Goodnight, fair sister." He opens his door and slips inside.

When the door closes, he leans against it and reaches into his pocket, pulling out the feather and blowing against it, it turns gold in his hand, and he smiles. "Such magic." the feather falls apart, and a piece of paper appears in his hand. He opens the folds gently and reads aloud. "Prince of the Sea, I wish to speak with you again. Meet me at this location." he frowns. "What location?" He turns the paper over, and a map appears. "By the sea." There is a red marker and a timestamp for the next day.

He turns to his wall and waves a hand. The wall clears to water as the fish swim beyond, and he holds the paper to the glass and smiles. "What does one do, Carapace?"

The sea turtle comes forward and nudges the glass. Carapace his familiar has been with him for twenty years now.

"Aye, brother." Leviathan pulls out the paperback and smiles. "What does one wear?" He turns to his closet. "He wore grey and gold, so- Blue?" the turtle turns away in the tank. "Silver? Perhaps green."

Carapace rolls over when he holds up the silver-lined dark coat. "Aye, Silver." he grabs out a black uniform with large cuffs and silver buttons. "This perfection."

Carapace bumps the glass, and Leviathan turns. "You wish to know of him! I shall tell you of him. His voice is calming, and soft; he has red hair, but not as red as my sisters. Skin like milk, eyes like stars...."

Carapace dances in the tank "Tomorrow." he nods, "Get some rest my friend." He waves a hand at the tank going dark. He turns to his bed and flops down with a smile. "So true a fool is love-" In that much, his dear friend Shakespeare had been right.

The following day Leviathan stands on a sandy beach near the water. He closes his eyes taking in a deep breath; the salty air is lovely. Gulls fly out over the water; it is a perfect day. "I hope this was alright." A voice causes him to turn around.

Raphael stands a few feet away in a white robe

with bare feet and hair down around his shoulders. "Indeed, perhaps there are better ways to get my attention."

"It worked, didn't it?"

"How did you make the feather combust?"

"A miracle; Gabriel and I used to use something similar to pass notes." He laughs, "when we were new." He shrugs, "When they, God, wasn't looking." He reaches up pushing long red locks behind his ears.

"Before the Great Divide?"

"Do you remember it?" Raphael asks softly.

"Aye, some of it, but Heaven, and our time, as there are hard memories to pull to attention. We were robbed of those memories." Leviathan reaches up, pulls his cap off his head, and nods. "The fall was painful, not something someone forgets." He fumbles with the rim of his hat. "But that is where our story stops. Little is known of before that time."

"What did you do before... What did you call it?"

Leviathan smiles, "The Great Divide, I sculpted rivers and seas, though exactly which I could not say, and how I could not tell." he says, "I helped them-" a gesture up, "With anything to do with water, but I know little else of my time above."

"Do you make ice?"

"Not I, t'was another angel." He shrugs. "I barely remember her, perhaps him. We didn't speak about that, I recall. Again, all memories of Heaven are blurry and faded. I do not trust them to be truthful recollections."

Raphael lifts his robe, stepping across the sand to enter the water. "You can control it?" He asks. "The water, the sea?"

"Yes, I can." Leviathan waves a hand, the water around Raphael's legs retreating before washing back. "I can control all water save for Holy water."

"With good reason, but Holy Water has a half-life. It doesn't just stay Holy Water forever." Raphael says softly. "Do you speak to the creatures of the seas as well?"

"Most, some dare not speaketh to me." He winks. "Angelfish particularly have a distaste for my presence."

Raphael laughs, "is this a joke?"

"A jest?" Leviathan asks. "You know of Jests, General?"

"Well, a few; Cassiel hears of them from the

watchers on earth, he tells us sometimes." Raphael steps further into the water.

Leviathan walks in with him and takes his elbow. "Easy, the tide of the ocean pulls," he says softly. "If you are unaware, thy feet may fall from beneath you."

"Well, good thing I have someone who commands the sea." Raphael smiles. "I-" He turns to Leviathan entirely. "I think about you with urgency."

"Speak." Leviathan is confused by the statement, "Why for?"

"I could not answer that," Raphael shrugs. "I simply cannot keep you out of my mind, and it makes no sense you are a Demon. You're damned, You speak so strangely, and yet-"

Leviathan smiles and touches his face. "And yet."

"Those rubies follow my mind. When I close my eyes, I see your eyes, hear your voice." Raphael frowns, "Are you tricking me? Is this some demonic enchantment?"

Leviathan laughs, "One does not enchant minds," he leans forward and whispers. "That would be my sister."

Raphael shakes his head. "I find myself uncomfortable, wanting, and yet, afraid to want."

"What is the source of thy discomfort?" Leviathan does not move when Raphael moves away.

"Me, my form, myself, everything, the world. Did you see the child?" Raphael turns, "A baby; you saw the baby today at the hearing." Leviathan can see the joy on his face. "It was amazing, so many new things- I am overwhelmed by the newness of it all, and I wonder if maybe I'm not thinking straight."

"I have seen them before," Leviathan says. "Children," he admits.

"I never have." Raphael turns to him. "I've not been to earth since-" He shrugs, "A few thousand years, and well I wasn't exactly allowed around people at the time."

Leviathan blinks, "That's a long time." He thinks hard and extends his hand. "Would you place your trust in me?"

"Why?" Raphael holds back.

"I wish to show you something that would bring tears to eyes," Leviathan says softly.

"You wish to make me cry?" Raphael looks confused.

"With joy." His hand extends to the angel closer.

Raphael steps back to him and takes his hand. "I trust you, Leviathan." They teleport away.

"You can call me Levi; Most do." he smiles as they arrive in a blink of an eye.

"Fast miracles." Leviathan smiles and turns Raphael around. "What is that?" Raphael steps forward, looking down at the ground before going ahead.

"That is a waterfall." Leviathan smiles.

Raphael walks forward and nearly trips on a stone in the river. Leviathan grabs his arm and steadies him with a smile. "I have thee." They hold their eyes for a long moment. "You are a difficult angel, aren't you?"

"That's what my brothers tell me." They get their footing. "Gabriel isn't my biggest fan. He says I am too sentimental."

"Does your High Commander know you are here?" Leviathan asks softly.

"Michael? I don't think so, and I didn't exactly tell him. He's gone off somewhere himself, not sure where." He waves a hand. "He goes to these sword things." Raphael rolls his eyes. "He collects weapons. I don't know maybe that has to do with being the Archangel of War."

"We all have weapons," Leviathan says. "I have a trident, though I find it cumbersome." He smirks. "What weapon doth thou wield?"

Raphael shrugs and opens his arms, a bow appearing, a quiver around his back. He grabs an arrow.

Leviathan laughs brightly. "Ranged combat." He seems pleased. "marvelous."

"I am a healer." Raphael says, "Heath and wellness, Michael insists I'm never going to be on the front lines of anything. That our weapons are merely for show, not for action. Michael wishes for us all to become masters of our weapons."

Leviathan frowns. "I like Michael's thinking, but Garbiel should have more faith." He points to the top of the waterfall giving a gentle wave of his hand. This causes the water from the fall to crash over the rocks beside the waterfall. "That middle rock there hit it." He puts his hat on his head and crosses his arms over his chest.

Raphael takes an arrow out of his quiver. He slides it against the bow and pulls back. Leviathan watches the spot until the released arrow hits it squarely. Raphael turns his head and smiles, "Happy?"

Leviathan smiles, "You're a marvelous shot."

"So don't anger me." Raphael turns back to him. "Or one might have to put an arrow in that heart of yours." He taps the bow against Leviathan's chest.

Silence covers both of them, "Perhaps one already has." Leviathan smiles, "I could never anger such beauty." he smiles. "Thine eyes are like the sun, thy hair like gentle earth...."

Raphael lowers his arms, but his hand covers his mouth. "Do you say such things to everyone?"

He shakes his head, "I could not, would not."

Leviathan reaches out, taking Raphael's free hand. "You have painted your nails with colors."

Raphael smiles. "Is it too much?"

"Nay." Leviathan smiles at him. "They are beautiful, gold like the sun, like the stars," a breathy pause, "like your eyes.." He leans forward, kissing the angel's knuckles. "You said you were worried that I had enchanted you."

"You said you hadn't." Raphael quips.

"I believe, sir, that you have enchanted me," Leviathan admits. "For I am so vexed by thine presence."

Raphael pauses, "Hell."

Leviathan smiles, "Hell, tis my name, Silver-fish."

"It is not." Raphael laughs deeply, but his face reddens at the name.

"This is folly." He says softly, but they are inching closer to one another, hands finding purchase against one another.

"Like it's crazy?" Raphael drops his bow to the ground.

"Aye, tis madness." Leviathan murmurs.

"Then let's be crazy." Raphael kisses him gently, chastely at first, and then with more fervor.

Leviathan opens his eyes to see the wings of the angel extended. "Oh-"

"Show me yours?" Raphael asks.

Leviathan nods and rolls his shoulder; his large black wings appear, with specks of white dancing on his primaries. "Does this please thee?"

"How beautiful." Raphael smiles. "I've never seen a demon's wings before."

"Most are black; some of us, like myself and Beelzebub, have little grey or white specks left." He says, "Beelzebub has the wings of a vulture." he smirks. "And I have no idea what these could be."

"A swan or a duck, perhaps?"

"A waterfowl?" Leviathan laughs. "Perhaps. Do it again, Silverfish."

"Do what?"

"Kiss me again," Leviathan says softly. "Again and again."

Raphael nods, "As much as you like."

"I would wish no other companion in eternity but you." Leviathan accepts that gladly and seals their mouths together.

XIII

Michael

"Discovery." Raguel sighs and drops a file in front of Michael.

"Watchers have records of seeing him for years in the same area," Phanuel adds.

Michael takes the file and flips the pages over. "These are Mathias' signatures." He sighs. "He knew that Nergal was making those visits for years." He sighs. "So what caused Mathias to attack this demon."

"That's not what we have to prove. We have to prove that Nergal killed Mathias, and there was the intent." Phanuel pipes up.

Raguel nods, "That- and we don't have a lot to go on."

"Does Hell get access to these?"

"Its Discovery, so yes," Raguel says. "But we get all their data too."

"What data do they have?" Michael asks.

"Nothing in the file for Nergal they sent that we didn't already know." Phanuel speaks up again, "Because well, they simply have to defend our attacks on them."

"Like Nergal did with Mathias?" Michael asks. "We need to know what instigated this if they knew one another, spoke to each other." Michael drops the file back on the table and stands. "Get me something else, there's little we can go on, and Death hates speculation."

"We know that, sir." Raguel sits down next to his brother.

"Who do you plan to question next?" Michael asks.

"We wish to question Cassiel, and then we want to have Beelzebub on the stand to question his leadership motives. Nergal was his."

Michael nods but still can't understand what questioning Beelzebub would do, but he doesn't object. He stands and grabs his jacket off the back of the chair. "Leave a note with my office; if you need something, I'll check back in."

"Where are you going, sir?"

"I have lots of responsibilities, not just those for this trial, gentlemen." He nods. "Again, if you need me, reach out. Call my office."

"Yes, sir." Phanuel stands, but his brother looks at him sternly, so he slowly sits back down.

Michael smiles. "Gentlemen." he exits the room and chuckles to himself, pulling the door closed.

"What's so funny?" Gabriel falls in step with him.

"Raguel and Phanuel are like oil and water." He laughs. "They don't get along, and they don't mix well."

"I mean, they know what they are doing." He says softly. "They're the best we have when it comes to the law that makes up these treaties."

"I don't disagree, but Raguel has a heavy hand." Michael shrugs.

"Not your style?" Gabriel laughs as they walk. "I find that hard to believe with as pushy as you can sometimes be."

"I am not pushy," Michael argues. "How are the halls?"

"They are lovely, lots of extra power, lots of new souls coming in. It's all going well. Numbers are right where they need to be."

"Anything strange?"

"No, but we did get a few infant souls that were a little strange, very powerful. We had to rebox them, but that happens from time to time."

"New Heavens?" Michael asks.

"Very Robust souls, it's in the file on your desk." Gabriel says, "I think Ariel has Cassiel calmed down now."

"I should check in on him."

"We have him. He's fine." Gabriel argues.

"He lost a man. As a host, he is not fine." Michael says, "Give him time. How are his animals?"

"As far as I know, he's back in his room, his forest." Gabriel sighs. "Animals too."

"Let him rest then." Michael nods, "Raguel and Phanuel do wish to question him."

"I dunno if that's a good idea." Gabriel sighs. "He sobs every time we bring it up."

"I'll work on that." Michael stalls his steps at

his door. "I'm gonna get a nap." He says, "I'm kinda tired."

"Sure, I can handle things up here." Gabriel pats his arm and moves down the hallway. Michael steps inside his room and closes the door before he waves a hand to change his clothes, and he teleports out of his room to Earth.

Michael is the first to arrive at the penthouse this time. He walks around and moves things. He uses a miracle to make sure a bottle of cognac is available, and he does lift the phone and follows the instructions to order Room service, their usual dinners just delivered to the room.

Beelzebub does arrive a few hours later. He walks through the door and smiles before closing the door behind him. "You picked up that quickly."

Michael smiles. "I have questions."

"I'm not talking about the baby." Beelzebub holds up his hands.

"It's not about that," Michael smiles. "But you were adorable." Beelzebub folds his arms over his chest, and Michael stands up and comes to him. "You smelt of Vanilla, and there was a buzzing, soft, but I could hear it."

Beelzebub nods and shucks out of his jacket and sits down in an oversized chair. "So, I am the Demon of Gluttony. Sometimes I can smell of vanilla, lavender, or sugar." He shrugs "the buzzing, well, I am the lord of the flies." he taps his arm. "You've seen the tattoo."

"I thought it was metaphorical."

"More like metaphysical." Beelzebub shrugs. "I buzz like a bee if I need to. It helps calm children, and some animals too."

"Your human name is Benjamin Hive." Michael smiles. "Like a buzzing beehive."

"Do you want a gold star for that impressive deduction?" Beelzebub smirks. "I chose it because it was easy." He reaches in his jacket pocket and tosses out a black leather wallet with ID cards and information. "I have all the relevant paperwork."

"Why?" Michael picks up the wallet. "Why would you want to pass as a human?"

"In case one day I have to, remember we aren't in Heaven downstairs." He smiles. "If souls stop coming, we're just as well off as the Hybrids are."

"My people want to put you on the stand," Michael says and leans back on the sofa, tossing the wallet back on the table.

Beelzebub picks it up and pockets it again, "I expected it." He gestures out. "Mine want to speak to Mathias' boss."

"I don't know if Cassiel is fit to take the stand," Michael says.

"May not have a choice." Beelzebub reminds him. "I only have a few hours." He says. "I can't be gone for long."

"Me either, so I ordered dinner. It's on its way up." Michael points. "Cognac for you."

"Miracles are real." Beelzebub smiles, "He can be taught."

"I just want you to be happy."

Beelzebub smiles, "Is that all?"

"Yes."

The knock comes from the door before more can be said, "Room service."

Beelzebub stands and gets out his wallet and pulls out some cash, "You have to give them money. It's called a tip." He suggests and opens the door. Michael watches Beelzebub give the man some money after leaving the tray. The man leaves, closing the door behind him.

Beelzebub reaches down to the plates and lifts them, taking them to the coffee table that divides the sitting room. Beelzebub sets them down before he removes silver toppers and returns them to the cart to bring back silverware and the drinks.

He steps across in the other direction to grab the cognac and two small glasses off the bar and the ice bucket. "Get started," he says and comes back.

Michael picks up his fork and picks at his fish. "If we take Nergal's life, Heaven would like to support Quilla and the child."

"How so?" Beelzebub asks, sitting down and using tongs to place ice into the glasses.

"She lives in Heavenly territories, and if we take away the one thing that has been a constant in her life, we will make sure she has nothing to worry about."

"And if she won't accept your help?" Beelzebub pours the cognac into two glasses before lifting his own to his lips and taking a sip. "What will you do? Just feel guilty forever?"

Michael takes a bite of his fish and chews while thinking. He swallows and shrugs. "I'm not sure. I just want to do what's right."

Beelzebub reaches across taking his free hand, and they eat like that in near silence. "Look, maybe we should stop this." He says, setting his fork down beside his food.

"Maybe," Michael says but discards his fork and stands, pulling Beelzebub along.

"I haven't finished my food." Beelzebub motions back.

"I don't care," Michael says and pushes him toward the bedroom. "I want you, I will have you, and you will agree."

Beelzebub smiles. "I can eat it later." He says of the food and turns into the bedroom. His eyes flash. "Shit." He covers them.

"What is it?" He looks the demon over. "What just happened to your eyes?"

Beelzebub looks nervous-looking this way and that. "I have to go. I can't explain." Beelzebub kisses him fiercely and fast before teleporting away.

Michael stands in the wake of it and sighs as he shakes his head. He looks over at the chair. He walks around and lifts Beelzebub's jacket, and smells deep. The smells are vanilla with floral notes. Michael decides that he can't leave the Jacket here. He folds the coat over his arm and Teleports back to his room in Heaven. Content to return it to Beelzebub the next time they're to meet. He lays the jacket over the arm of his armchair but notes something in the pocket. He reaches in and pulls out the silver cigarette case and the lighter. "Oh no." He turns to his desk and grabs a manilla envelope, and slides them inside. He addresses the package and lifts it, addressed to Hell. With any luck, it will go straight to Beelzebub.

He'll make sure the jacket is returned by hand. He sighs, starts to sign a few forms waiting for him in his IN box, and drops them in his OUT box where they vanish. He closes his eyes and leans back in his chair, and shakes his head. "Why is this so hard?" He sighs. A knock comes to his door, and perhaps it's best he's returned. "Enter."

Raphael walks in and shuts the door slowly behind him. "Hey, can I talk to you?"

"About what?" Michael clears his desk.

"Cassie." He smiles. "Raguel came and asked him to testify."

"There's not much I can do about that," Michael says softly and shrugs. "You look different."

Raphael reaches up and pushes his long hair behind his ears. His nails are showing. "Frigg helped me with some things for the trial, and I think I like them."

"Nail paints and Jewelry?" Michael smiles. "It's nice to see you smile. You haven't for a long time."

"Life has been very monotonous as of late, and while I would never wish Mathias dead, this has just allowed us to be away from Heaven in ways we haven't been before."

Michael nods, "I know."

"I went to Earth."

"You did?" That is surprising, and it's been ages since Raphael last went.

"I saw a waterfall." He smiles, "It was beautiful."

"Most of God's creation is beautiful," Michael says. "Some of it is capable of great evil, but some of it is just pure."

"Like a waterfall?"

"Like a waterfall. A canyon may be something you might like to see too; the sights can be amazing," Michael smirks. "I like the food sometimes as well, the music on occasion."

Raphael turns to the TV and VCR on the table. "You like their films too." he gestures to the shelves covered in movies and books.

"Mostly informational ones called documentaries, that speak of real-world events," he explains.

"We keep our hands out, but I like knowing what happened even if I wasn't there."

"You do?" Raphael beams, "For being best friends, I feel like I don't know you half as well as I should." He laughs, "What sorts of foods do you eat when you are there?"

"Wine, fish, sometimes cake." Michael looks up, "There are these fried potatoes." He groans a bit.

Raphael frowns, "Humans can eat fish?"

"Humans, Demons, Hybrids, all can eat almost any creature in one form or another. There are exceptions to that rule, but yes."

"I want to know more about the earth."

"Cassiel would be a good place to start. His people are all over it." He motions to his television. "There are some videos I can show you, but they don't do the places any justice. You really must see them with your own eyes."

"Why doesn't Cassie go to Earth?"

"I don't know." Michael shrugs, "Never thought to ask him."

"Perhaps we should." Raphael beams at him.

Michael smiles in agreement. "I think you might be right."

XIV

Beelzebub

Beelzebub appears in smoke in the throne room. His thoughts are all of Michael up there alone in the penthouse. "So he can come when summoned," Lucifer says softly. "I want an update on what is going on with the trial." Lucifer stands up and walks over to him.

Beelzebub swallows his pride and nods, walking forward. "They're taking 48 hours to do what they call Discovery, to go over watcher records. Nergal has been seeing his daughter at this location for a long time, Father. There's a question as to why Mathias would have attacked him now."

"So, how does it look thus far?" Lucifer asks.

"Right now? I think we have a firm hold on some of this; we may be able to spare his life if we can't spare his freedom." Beelzebub explains.

"I have the requests from their lawyers. They want you to testify." He hands over a paper. "I have already approved it."

Beelzebub nods. "Of course." He says softly. "Nergal is part of my legion. It would be right to question me."

"They are also going to question the angel in charge of Mathias. Cassiel." He says softly. "Cassie, when I knew him was meek and small, he may be much the same."

"You're saying we might be able to win this because he won't have the conviction to testify?"

"I'm not saying anything, Beelzebub. You and the others, your memories of Heaven, are so foggy. I remember Heaven. Every moment. You, my children, don't." Lucifer stands up shoving his hands in his pockets. "That is a blessing, I assure you. I have spoken with your mother." He says, head canting to one side as if trying to study Beelzebub's face for a reaction.

Beelzebub puts the folder under his arm and

suddenly realizes he doesn't have his jacket. His cigarette case and lighter are in the breast pocket. "About what?" He shrugs.

"She says you've gotten attached to someone," Lucifer says with a beaming smile, "Care to tell me who?"

"Not really." Beelzebub folds his arm across his chest, defensive.

"And if I ordered you?" Lucifer's tone goes dark. It's a serious question.

Beelzebub looks at him and tilts his head. "I don't think you would. Mother would forbid it." He's confident his mother would not allow that power to push between them. It wouldn't look right to anyone. Mother has always said they have to keep disputes to a minimum.

Lucifer laughs gently, "You know us too well, son. She already forbade me from ordering you to say." He sighs, "But don't let it keep you from what is important here. After this is over, I'm sure we can spare you some time away, but right now-"

"The trial is more important, I understand."

Lucifer nods, "Beelz." he motions Beelzebub closer, and the prince comes to his king. "I trust you with this more than anyone you know."

"Yes, father."

"Don't let me down." Lucifer walks away out of the back door of the throne room. Beelzebub lets out the breath he'd been holding.

A demon enters from the Hallway. "Your Highness?"

Beelzebub turns, "Yes, Otis isn't it?"

The demon smiles, "Close, your highness, my name is Botis."

"Apologies, Botis," He smiles. "It's been a long day. How can I help you?"

"Duke Lucas requires you in his office at your soonest convenience, Highness." Botis hands him a small note. "It's not a rush, but he'd like to speak to you when you're free."

Beelzebub turns the folder over in his hand. "I need to stop in my room for a moment. Please let the Duke know I'll be on my way shortly."

"Yes, your highness." Then Botis leaves him.

Beelzebub walks into his room and tosses the file to his table before walking to his closet to grab another jacket and a small golden case sitting on the shelf by the mirror. He looks inside it. It's got smokes and a lighter, so he pockets them.

Hopefully, he will find time to return to the hotel to grab his jacket.

He pulls on the new jacket with deep red lapels and smirks at himself in the mirror, a hand reaching up to comb through his stringy black hair before he grabs the file back off the table and heads out to find Lucas.

"They're going to ask if you ordered this, Highness."

Beelzebub leans back, shaking his head, "Heaven already established that Mathias attacked Nergal." He waves a hand. "I did not order this." He holds out his hands. "Why would they think I ordered this? If Mathias was the one who engaged first."

"They will ask if you can feel where your subordinates are if you know what they're thinking." Lucas turns around to sit, his cat jumping onto the top of the table and lying down. "Hey, sweetheart."

"Is that your familiar?" Beelzebub asks.

"Yes." He nods, "I've had her with me for a long time." He turns to another file. The black cat eyes Beelzebub with dark yellow eyes. "Raguel is brutal in his questioning. He will try to catch you in things." Lucas says, drawing Beelzebub's attention away from the cat. "Please be mindful, highness, about what you disclose."

"I'll not make it easy for him," Beelzebub says. "It's not like I could know every thought and notion that goes through my Legionair's heads. If I did, we wouldn't have to talk like this."

"Your highness, we don't have much of a case to save Nergal. Outside of the obvious, the wrong place and time, he'd been going there for over sixty years." He sets out the angelic log. "It's all in ink and signed by Mathias. That was his territory to watch as a watcher, and it's been fine until recently."

"So, the question is-" Beelzebub shrugs. "What was the relationship between Mathis and Nergal?" He flips pages. "And when did it suddenly change?"

"That's a good question." Lucas nods. "That's a damned fine question." He makes a few notes. He stands up. "I think I have a few ideas of what to ask their General."

"Cassiel, yes?"

"That's the one, sir." Lucas reaches around himself to pull down another file from a shelf. Beelzebub notes a sword is hanging on the wall.

"What sort of weapon is that? Looks like Leviathan's sword a bit."

Lucas stalls, turning back. "Ah, it's called a Spadroon. And Leviathan's sword is not his relic weapon, highness; it's just a fancy sword he got on earth; it's Polish, I believe." He smiles. "Szabla, if I'm not mistaken."

"Are you ever mistaken?" Beelzebub chuckles.

"No sir, I never am when it comes to swords." Lucas opens a folder laying out a few things. "When you and Michael negotiated these treaties, were you ever given a list of watchers for angelic territories?"

"No." Beelzebub shakes his head.

"We don't have demons assigned to our territories, do we?"

"We do not and don't have demons just standing on earth. We're not paranoid like Angels are. We don't have the staffing for that." Beelzebub sighs.

"I think I have an idea of what we can do." Lucas is scribbling notes in his notebook.

"Do you need any help with this from anyone else? I don't want that team of angels ganging up on you." Beelzebub says firmly. "We need to try to save Nergal's life."

"I know, sir." Lucas looks up at him, "And we will."

Beelzebub looks at the table. "Why do I have doubts?"

Lucas looks up at him and stops everything he's doing. "Your Highness?"

"Yes?" Beelzebub blinks but looks up, meeting his eyes.

"We'll win this. I'll see to it."

"And if we don't?"

"You can forfeit my life instead of Nergal's." Lucas, noble Lucas, would mean such things. The duke stands and bows.

"Not happening." Beelzebub stands, pointing Lucas back to his seat, "Sit back down; see if I can get an audience with Nergal. He's in my legion, and I want to speak to him."

Lucas sits and scoots forward, "I will put in the request now, but I don't know if Heaven will allow it," Lucas says and grabs a form from another pile. His office does look like organized chaos in its natural state, and perhaps they need a little bit of that right now. One can't be sure.

"They'll allow it," Beelzebub says with certainty.

Lucas looks up at him as if trying to see through him. "Highness?"

"Keep working, Lucas." Beelzebub stood up and headed for the door. "Let me know when they respond to my request."

"Of course, Your Highness." Lucas stands and bows, and Beelzebub leaves the room.

XV

Michael

Michael looks at the reports on his desk, and another paper ends up in his inbox. He sighs and reads the form. "What's that one?" Cassiel is sitting across from him.

"It's a request to allow Beelzebub to meet with Nergal."

"Are you going to allow it?"

"If it were one of your watchers on trial and you wanted to speak with them, I would hope the demons would say yes," Michael says. "Beelzebub is the leader of Negal's Legion."

"Beelzebub is his Host?" Cassiel asks.

"Basically, yes." Michael smiles, "What do you think I should do?"

"I say you should let him. If there's a chance we win and he is destroyed, he should be able to see his host before he is nothing." his voice cracks, but he clears his throat. Cassie pets through the ears of his rabbit gently.

"That is very merciful of you, Cassie." Michael smiles at him brightly over the table's edge. "Why do you think he deserves this mercy?"

Michael folds his arms over the paperwork on his desk, giving the other angel his full attention.

"Mercy is for the wicked, brother." Cassiel still looks sorrowful. "But I would want the same benefit if Mathias had done this. You are correct, so please allow it."

"I shall, and I shall oversee it myself to make sure nothing untoward goes on, alright?"

"If Raguel will let you." Cassiel almost smiles but looks into his lap where a few small animals sleep in a pile, a rabbit, a hamster, and a guinea pig. There's a small sort of yellow bird on his shoulder.

"Raguel hasn't an option with me. I am his

host." Michael signs off and timestamps the paper-work, then drops it in the outbox to Hell.

"What about Phanuel?" Cassie asks.

"Gabriel is his host." Michael chuckles. "Can't think we would put both our Lawyers under the same host, did you?" Michael looks back through his paperwork, signing off on something else, dropping it in the outgoing bin.

Cassiel looks away from the desk. "You don't have to do this, you know."

"Do what?" He's barely listening right now. He's got a lot on his mind.

"Watch me like I'm going to break," Cassiel mutters.

That makes him look up and stop everything. "That's not what this is."

"It isn't?" Cassiel shrugs. "I overheard Gabriel talking about keeping me occupied so I wouldn't be so upset."

Michael frowns, "I'm sorry. We didn't know what else to do."

Another form pops into Michael's inbox, and he nearly disregards it. He sighs and grabs it up, and sits back in his chair. "They want you to testify."

"Me?"

"Yes, Hell's barrister is asking for you." He lays the form out for Cassiel to view.

"I suppose I always knew that was going to happen." Cassiel takes the form in his hand and sighs. "Okay."

"You're sure you're okay with this?" Michael has to ask him. Not doing so would be irresponsible.

"Yes." He nods gently.

Michael turns to the side of his desk, lifts the receiver on his desk phone, and presses one of the buttons at the bottom. "Get Raguel and Phanuel to my office, please." He nods. "Thank you." He hangs up.

"Why?"

"They will need to coach you on your answers."

"Isn't that deceitful?"

"No, what I mean is, they will ask you the questions they believe Hell will ask you, and with them, you will be able to answer more easily and more readily. Think of it as trying to answer hard questions before you have to. Practice."

"Practice?" Michael nods at him, "When you put it that way, that sounds reasonable." Michael smiles. He needs Cassiel to do this.

"I'm glad you think so." Michael stops and looks across at him, "Heaven would never ask you to be deceitful, Cassie."

"Okay." He attempts a small smile, but Michael can see this is breaking his heart.

The trial resumes the next day. Fully rested, Micahel is the first angel to arrive, one hour before proceedings start. When he does, he notes Beelzebub and his lawyer are already there. "Are you ready to speak with Nergal, your highness?"

"Not without oversight." The echo breaks off anything Beelzebub is to say as Death appears on the high platform above everything.

"Of course, you are welcome to stand watch as I do," Michael says.

"Then come; you will have ten minutes." Death motions the two to a door on the side of the courtroom. It opens, and Beelzebub looks briefly at Michael before turning for the door. Death vanishes.

Michael follows Beelzebub into the room, and Death is already standing in the corner.

"Boss?" Nergal is in his cage, but he stands up. He sees Death and Michael. "What's going on?" He bows his head. "Your highness..." It's brought up very last for some reason, and Michael watches, perplexed.

"You asked for me," Beelzebub says, standing beside the bars. "Didn't you?"

"Yeah, I just-" he reaches into his pocket, and a sound comes from Death's shroud. "It's just a watch, sir." He shows it to Death and says, "I want him to give it to my daughter, just in case."

Death comes forward and looks at the watch; it opens without being touched, and Death nods. "Is this acceptable to Heaven?"

Michael nods, "Perfectly acceptable to leave a child an heirloom." Michael looks over at Nergal; he hasn't seen him up close. He's not listening to whatever conversation he has with Beelzebub because something has caught his eye. He walks up to the bars; something behind the demon's ears makes him stall. "Nergal?"

Death turns to him. "You are not free to speak now; just listen." Nergal is handing the pocket watch to Beelzebub, who puts it into his trousers pocket.

"No, Death, you misunderstand." The shroud

comes to Michael and towers over him. "Look, just there, behind his ear." Michael turns his head, lifting his hair to show the shroud of his marking. "He's a horseman like we are." Death looks him up and down, and Michael turns his head, pulling a few strands to show the shroud of his mark.

Death's face turns, and Nergal's hair moves on his head unbidden. The horseshoe is unmistakable behind his ear. The same place where Michael and Beelzebub have their marks. "Pestilence." Beelzebub smacks the bars. He steps away from the cage. "Fuck."

"What?" Nergal looks around. "What is going on? I demand you explain yourselves."

"You are a horseman and thus cannot be put to death." Death says commandingly, moving through the cage bars to examine the demon closely. "Your fate is not yet written."

"We are the four horsemen," Michael says, looking between them. "War." He points to himself. "Death." The shroud. "Famine." He points to Beelzebub. "And Pestilence," Nergal looks himself up and down. "You are the horseman that brings disease to the land."

Beelzebub leans against the far wall. "What do we do?" He opens his hands. "This isn't gonna look good if we just stop the trial now."

Michael looks at Death. "Nergal cannot put him to death, so what are our options?" He looks at the door. "What do we say to everyone?"

"I must check death records for a moment." Death looks between them all. "Do not leave one another. Stay here." He vanishes.

"That's just fucking grand!" Beelzebub yells, "COME BACK HERE!"

"Your highness, please." Nergal turns to Michael. "You said Disease?" He blinks and looks at the door. "Does that- you're sure?"

"Yes." Michael nods. "It's the only one you can be." He motions to Beelzebub, "Famine is ...what will happen if Beelzebub's true nature of Gluttony takes hold." He nods, "I will bring war and violence to the end times."

"I did it." Nergal says softly, looking at his hands, "It was me."

"Does this mean something to you?" Belzebub asks. "You act as though this explains something for you."

"My daughters' children, well, they die young,"

He frowns. "From sickness, and we-" He shrugs, "Is it me?" Nergal looks from Beelzebub to Michael. "Am I killing my grandchildren?"

"It's quite possible." Michael nods. "Until death returns, there's not much we can do."

"Jesus Christ." Beelzebub sighs. "What do we fucking do?"

"You need to calm down," Michael says firmly.

"How can I when Heaven wants him dead, and they can't have what they want?" Beelzebub frowns at him, and damn if Michael doesn't want to kiss him even as angry as he is. "They'll want my head next, and they can't have that either."

"We just have to let the trial go on. Death is ultimately the one who will call their judgment." Michael shrugs. "Maybe we do this dance, go through it, and then...maybe Death lets him off."

"I killed an angel." Nergal says, "If Death were to let me off, Heaven wouldn't accept it."

"You're probably right." Michael agrees.

"I didn't mean to kill him," Nergal says kindly. "It wasn't supposed to end like that-"

"Yes, well, you killed, and we can't kill you in return for it. God has plans for you." Michael sighs, "for all of us."

Beelzebub sighs. "You're the demon of the fig tree." He says softly. "A plant elemental."

"Yes, sir, your highness, I thought that was my lot in life, but I'm killing people-" he nods, and his head bows low. He lifts his hand and holds out a fig. He looks between them now, faces pale. Michael can see now even the most beautiful flowers have thorns.

Beelzebub takes the fig into his hand and stares at it. Michael comes around the cell, "What are you thinking, Bee?"

"Your highness is his title, Angel," Nergal says. "You will respect him."

Michael can't respond before Beelzebub speaks, "He does respect me. He may call me what he wishes." Michael swells with pride at the statement.

"Beelzebub," The demon meets his eyes, "Meet me. Five years from today, Paris," Michael says softly.

"Five years from today." Beelzebub agrees. "Our usual time, don't be late."

"What's that supposed to mean?" Nergal asks. "Your Highness, what is he talking about?"

Before they can answer, Death reappears, "We

as horsemen overrule Heaven and hell in judgment; we can decide." He motions between them. "We can make the determination, and it can stand due to our status."

"Heaven cannot know I'm a horseman." Michael insists. "They'll lock me up, hold me hostage. It's why I've never once said, and I keep my mark hidden."

"Lucifer knows about me, but no one in Hell knows about Nergal. Those that do are in this room," Beelzebub admits. "Death, what do you think we should do about this?"

"We let him escape." The shroud says, "but it must look good, and you must be able to part ways when we leave this place. I will bear witness that you both intended to stop him." He floats to the cage.

"Brother." Death opens the door. "Flee, do not be found, do not return to your daughter."

"Fill this place with vines, wrap us up, and you're gonna have to harm us a little bit," Beelzebub says. "Make it look good, do some damage." He takes his jacket off, tears the arm from the coat's body, and tosses it down.

Michael nods and undoes his tie a bit. He

reaches back, pulling the elastic band out of his hair to shake it out, using a hand to rough it up. "Death, could you do the honors?" He says, "Bruise us up?"

"I will, but be warned. This will cause a rift between Heaven and Hell for many years." Death says, "You will have to be torn away to avoid suspicion." The shroud comes to Michael and touches his face leaving a bruise, and Michael winces. A force pushes into Michael's chest, and he groans, nearly dropping to his knees.

Michael turns his head, meeting Beelzebub's eyes. "We know," he rasps out. He watches as Death motions Nergal into the open. "You will go here." He touches Nergal on the forehead. "I will meet you." seeming to impart a location without saying where.

"That's not very far." Nergal looks between them. "Are you sure?"

"I am. You were for me, will be for me, are for me." The shroud says. "Thus, you will meet me there." Death wraps his bone-like hand around the fly mark on Nergal's arm, and it melts off like liquid, replaced with a skull. "I take you as one of mine, as is my right."

Nergal rolls his neck and reaches into his pocket, pulling out seeds, acorns, and figs, tossing them down on the ground as if sorting them before keeping hold of a few sources in his hand. "Redwood ought to do it, with some kudzu and more vines, yes...Jungle vines...."

Death nods, "once it starts, vanish." He insists. "Best get on the other side of the room, Archangel. If they find you two speaking, the sides will have questions."

"Five years, Bee." Michael reminds him.

"Five years." Beelzebub agrees.

Death forces Michael across the room, slamming him into the wall. "Now, Nergal." Death's voice echoes through the ringing in Michael's ears. He slides to the ground holding his side face contorted in pain. He forces his eyes open to watch.

Plants fill the room, and vines snake around him. He summons his sword to fight back the growth, to look like they're attempting to stop it. Michael scrambles to his feet, still holding his side, chopping at the long vines. Death is gone; somehow, he vanished when it started.

Beelzebub is almost out of sight at this point. Nergal also seems to be gone. The room-filling is faster than he can seem to keep track of a tall tree in the center where the cell had been, and vines fill almost everything else. A demon making a garden looks so strange to Michael, but then again, everything has been weird since he walked into this room.

Beelzebub is cutting his way through small patches with his daggers. "MICHAEL!" The demon prince is attempting to fight the vines, to get to him, but the room is filling up with plant life fast.

"Stay there, Bee!" Michael insists they have to stay separated, and with the thick growth, it might be a while before their people can dig them out. "Hell." He mutters as the vines snake around his legs and squeezes hard enough to break even angelic bones. He lets out a scream he can't keep hold of and drops to the ground. He can hear Beelzebub scream again. Michael's heart breaks listening to that voice in any amount of pain.

XVI

Raphael

"I promise it shouldn't be that bad; once Michael is done overseeing the demons, the trial will start. Do you feel prepared?" Raphael stops them just inside the courtroom and smiles at him.

Cassiel looks at him and nods. "I think so." Small mice peek out of Cassiel's pockets.

"Good." Raphael gives him a pat on the back. He's proud of how Cassiel is taking this responsibility.

"General." Raguel comes in with a smile on his bright face. "Generals, I should say good morning to you both."

"Hello there, Raguel, and good morning to you as well," Raphael looks around a moment, "Where is your counterpart?"

"Speaking with his host." He thumbs a finger over at the door. "Gabriel stopped him before he could walk in here; not sure what for, but that's between an angel and his host, I suppose."

"Speaking of, have you seen Michael yet?" Raphael asks. "or was he supposed to come later?"

"Should have been here already to oversee the demon speaking with the Crown Prince." Raguel sets a few things on his table. "Was my understanding that he would be present as well as Death for that conversation." He shakes his head. "It should have been the councilors, but Death rejected my request."

There is a rumbling, and the room begins to shake. "What's that!?" Cassiel backs into Raphael, scared. The room lurches, and Cassiel falls into Raphael's arms to keep his balance.

"I don't know." Raphael turns to Raguel.

"What magic be this?" Leviathan rushes into the room, sword drawn, the Demonic councilor Lucas beside him, his weapon also at the ready. "Be this the work of Heaven?" He asks sternly. "I pray thee angels, speak!"

"We don't know, your Highness," Raphael speaks and keeps a hold of Cassiel. "Give us a moment. We're just as confused as you are."

"General." Raguel points to the door beside the pedestal where Death should have been sitting for the trial. Vines and things are growing out from under the crack in the door. "That's not good," he says, backing up slightly and stepping onto his chair as the vines start to cover the floor and grass grows beneath their feet. A scream draws their attention to the door that begins to break as more vines start to slither into the open.

"That was Michael!" Raphael looks back as Gabriel enters the room with Phanuel. "Gabriel!" Raphael points at the door.

Gabriel pushes through and looks at the demons. "Is Michael in there?" He turns that question to Raphael's finger, pointed squarely in the doorway.

"I think so. I heard Michael scream." She turns to Phanuel, "Take Cassiel back to Heaven."

"General-" Phanuel steps forward in protest.

"That's an order, soldier." Raphael barks and then glances at Leviathan.

"This is Hell's doing," Gabriel mutters, manifesting his sword from the air. "We'll see you destroyed for this."

Leviathan, Raphael is thankful and holds his tongue. "We don't know that, Gabriel!" Raphael says firmly keeping a footing between the two.

Another scream makes Leviathan visibly jump. "Beelzebub, my dear brother."

"What if it is both?" Lucas argues, stepping up on a chair next to Raguel when the Vines start to climb him. "What if they're destroying one another?"

"We will go in together.... Side by side." Raphael says and reaches behind himself, pulling his bow from nothing. "Your highness." He motions to Leviathan, who comes forward with his sword and starts to hack at the vines as they push toward the doorway. Raphael stays behind his back, Gabriel just behind them, and Lucas follows.

"'Tis thicker than the jungles of South America!" He growls, "Hold fast" Leviathan holds up a hand to stop anyone going forward. "I shall make way for us." He fists his hand, and the vines start to wither. Water flows out of them and onto his arm before trickling upwards. Water begins to flow out of all the plants growing up the walls retaining a spot near the ceiling. Raphael watches with awe. "Cut them now while I have them droughted. Tis the only way."

Gabriel doesn't waste any time pushing ahead of the demon and Raphael to look around the room. "Michael?" He starts to cut his way through the vines and climb over massive roots. Raphael looks left and right when his eyes fall upon Beelzebub, slumped over on his side. Raphael puts a hand over his mouth.

Raphael looks back at Leviathan and pauses before he swallows. "We'll get him, find thine own brother." Leviathan is insistent. He looks at Lucas, "Fetch the crown." He stands still, arms tangled in the vine as he works. "I can hold the water from the vines, but I must remain here."

Raphael stalls briefly but departs into the room, stepping over large dying vines, the leaves cracking under his feet. He turns, seeing Gabriel kneeling and a pair of legs. "Michael." He rushes over to where the angel lay against the wall, chest heaving—Sword at his side.

"The demons did this-" Gabriel growls as he pulls the vine away from Michael's body. "Say the word, and I will smite them all this moment in the lord's name."

"Beelzebub tried to capture him." Michael says, "It was just Nergal planning his escape; the Prince didn't know, couldn't have known." Michael says, holding his side. "Nergal attacked us both."

"Where is Death, wasn't he supposed to be here with you?" Gabriel looks at Raphael, who only shrugs; he doesn't know about that. Raphael is too busy working on pulling vines away from Michael's legs.

"Summoned away, I suppose that allowed Nergal to attempt-" Michael looks exhausted. "Well, to escape." Raphael cups his chin and looks at the bruising on his face. "I'm alright."

"No, you are not." Raphael kneels closer to get a better look at him, "Broken arm, shoulder, leg." He looks at Gabriel. "We can argue about whose fault this is at another time. We need to get him back upstairs." Raphael closes his eyes and channels some of his holy power into Michael, who looks relieved by the motion. "I can only dull his pain. He needs to be in Heaven."

Gabriel nods. "Let's go." He takes Raphael's hand. "We'll have words tomorrow, Demon." He glares at Leviathan in the doorway, who only seems to sheath his sword and stand there. The demonic lawyer carries their Prince in his arms and vanishes with him.

"I look forward to it, messenger." Leviathan turns his head to Raphael. "General Raphael."

Gabriel releases Raphael's hand. Lifting Michael in his arms, Gabriel vanishes with him. Raphael knows he should follow, but he stands looking around to make sure they are alone. "I love thee." a whisper barely a note in the air, but Raphael turns to Leviathan's voice. "Thine heart is but all I live for, dearest Raphael. I hope your brother heals quickly." Their fingers brush barely. It's all Raphael can do to hold himself back. "I promise nothing will happen between the Messenger and myself."

"And I love you, Levi; Heaven sends its best regards for Prince Beelzebub's quick healing," Raphael says but pulls back. "I'll talk to Gabriel, okay?"

"Will your beauty ever grace my eyes again?" Leviathan asks, voice just above a whisper, cracking.

"I-"Raphael shakes his head, "I don't know."

Leviathan reaches forward and pulls Raphael into his arms, embracing him tightly. "I love thee."

Raphael looks up, "You're a fool."

"Indeed." He kisses Raphael, "Go-"He says. "I must go too." Raphael steals another deep kiss.

"I'll try to get away. Two days from now, at dawn." Raphael says, backing away. "At the waterfall."

Leviathan bows, "My heart, I will be there." He vanishes, and Raphael does the same, destination Heaven.

Once in Heaven, he reaches up to the right of his hair. Working to control his emotions before he goes further down the hallway. "Where did Gabriel take the High Commander?" He stops an angel in the corridor.

An angel, Tauriel, points down the hallway. "To his room, sir." He bows to Raphael before he continues.

"Many thanks." Raphael rushes toward Michael's room, where Phanuel, Raguel, and Cassiel wait outside. "Go to your rooms, rest, and I will tell you when there is more to tell." She nods. Raguel looks like he doesn't want to go. "Your host is alive. I assure you I will let you know what is going on, but I must see to him first, dismissed."

Cassie comes to Raphael and hugs him tightly before turning away with the lower-ranked angels, who bookend him as if protecting him as they go. Small animals begin to come out of small hiding places in the hallway and follow them.

Raphael knocks before entering the room where Gabriel sits beside Michael, lying in his recliner chair. "Gabriel, will you go get a bottle of rose water? I think that should help his pain a little while I reset his bones."

"Angels should not be able to be harmed like this," Gabriel mutters and stands.

"Well, we can be by others of our kind," Raphael says, taking the vacated seat and taking Michael's hand.

"They are no longer our kind," Gabriel says firmly, folding his arms over his chest. "They are outcasts."

Raphael ignores Gabriel's protests as he meets Michael's eyes. "You look-"

"Like hell?" Michael adds.

"Don't say that here." Gabriel laughs and turns,

"I'll get a bottle or two of the Rosewater and be back soon." He pats Raphael's shoulder before leaving out the door.

"What do we do with you, hum?" Raphael stands up a little, taking his arm and rolling it. Michael flinches but the shoulder sets. "There we go."

He turns his attention to Michael's leg and holds a hand over it. "It'll be a few days before we have you up and moving around again." Michael nods. "You need to let me and Gabriel handle the day-to-day dealings."

"We need to find Nergal," Michael says.

"Gabriel can have Cassie get the watchers on it." Raphael smiles at him, "but right now, you have yourself to worry over." Michael takes his hand. Raphael looks up at him. "What is it?"

"Thank you."

"You're welcome; now rest." Raphael smiles at him, "We'll get through this." Raphael hopes they will.

"Gabriel wants to go to war," Michael says softly. "Attack Hell head-on."

Raphael frowns, "No, and you have my vote against that, you said that the Prince tried to stop

Nergal, that's all I need to know, and he was worse off looking than you by the looks of his injuries. Only God knows if he will survive them," Michael closes his eyes, "Is something wrong?"

"No, but I want to send a letter to Hell. Would you be able to take a note for me?" Michael squeezes his hand.

"Of course." Raphael smiles, "After I see these bruises." He touches Michael's face, and the bruising backs away from the skin. "It'll still hurt, mind you, but others won't have to see it." he beams. "I'm glad you're okay."

"Me too," Michael says softly. "Me too; if Hell sends anything up, I want to see it immediately, and if you hear from Death, you're to bring him straight here."

"Brother-"

"I want to speak to Death personally."

Raphael can only smile at him and nod, "Okay." He reaches up, pushing the blonde hair out of Michael's face. "You're getting shaggy."

"Would you cut it for me? Get it out of my eyes?" Michael asks.

"Of course." Raphael beams at him.

Gabriel walks in with two bottles and three glasses. "I thought, perhaps. We could all use a drink."

Raphael chuckles, "I think so too." He sits back. "Pop the cork, and let us be as we once were."

XVII

Beelzebub

Beelzebub wakes with a splitting headache. "Don't try to move, dear." He palms over his face groaning deeply, "You need not move so much."

"Mother?" He groans, opening his eyes.

"Yes, I'm here. Remington has seen your wounds. You need to rest." She stands and helps him sit up. "Would you like some tea? Perhaps a cookie? Chocolate? A donut?"

"Give him some room, Dear. You'll suffocate him." Lucifer enters with Hauster behind him, carrying a tray and setting it on the table beside the bed. "Thank you, Hauster, that will be all."

"Majesties," He says and looks at Beelzebub, "Highness."

Beelzebub waits until Hauster is out of the room. "We have to find Nergal."

"Can you summon him back?" Lucifer asks.

Beelzebub pulls the sleeve up on his arm and closes his eyes; the fly tattoo brightens, but nothing happens. "I'm calling, but he isn't responding."

"He's simply ignoring it." Lucifer sighs.

"No, Father," Lucifer turns to meet his eyes, "I'm sending, but it's not like he's not listening. Nothing is coming back to me." Beelzebub touches his head and groans a bit. "It's like he's not there."

"Has he been destroyed?" Lucifer asks him.

"I don't know. How long have I been unconscious?" He looks up at his mother. "Uh, my head-"

Lilith reaches out and touches his face. "A few days. Levi has been beside himself."

"Is he okay?" Beelzebub frowns.

"Yes, but he needed time to think, so he's left for the evening." She smiles. "Asmodeus is on the throne in your place, currently seeing things."

Beelzebub nods and leans back. "He just. Nergal, I mean-" he clutched his head, "he dropped these seeds, and they started to grow, and I tried to stop him, but he wouldn't listen to my orders."

"Then what happened?"

"The vines were so thick, after a few seconds, I lost sight of him before I became completely entangled."

"And where was Death in all this?" Lucifer comes to sit on the bed.

"He was there at the start, and then he left. Maybe he chased Nergal? I don't know." Beelzebub fishes in his pocket and pulls out a pocket watch. "Nergal wanted this to go to his daughter, Quilla."

Lucifer takes the timepiece and turns it over in his hand. "We'll see that it makes its way home." He insists.

"Have Remington look at her child," Beelzebub says softly.

"Why?" Lilith asks.

"She keeps losing her children in early years if she's lost her father-"

Lilith looks at Lucifer, and Beelzebub notes their faces. "I don't usually ask for things."

"I'll see to it personally," Lilith says with a smile. "We'll make sure the child is cared for."

"If Death shows up."

"I'll handle it." Lucifer nods.

"I want to be there. I want to hear what Death has to say." Beelzebub says. "If he destroyed Nergal, we must let Heaven know that."

"Alright, I'll send Death a summons." Lucifer pats his arm and stands. "Come, my love, dinner."

Lilith stands but leans over and kisses Beelzebub's forehead. "Remington will be in soon, and we'll have Hauster bring in some supper for you. We love you, Beelz."

"Thank you, mother. I love you too." She's the only one he says it to because it is true. He does love them; they have always cared for him.

Lucifer and Lilith leave him in his bed. He lays his head back a moment before turning to look at the tray hauster brought. The tray contains tea, coffee, cookies, donuts, and a manilla envelope. He shifts up and reaches for the envelope, and turns it over.

There is no postage, just his name written beautifully on the outside of the envelope. He knows the handwriting. He reaches up and tears it open, dumping the contents onto his lap. His silver cigarette case and lighter fall out. He chuckles and looks inside the envelope before reaching in; he finds no note. "Thanks, handsome." He says little else but saves the envelope aside.

He opens the case, pulls out a cigarette, puts it in his mouth, and lights it by taking a long draw. He blows the smoke out his nose and smiles brightly. "Five years." He murmurs.

Reaching the bedside drawer, he pulls it open, pulls out a small schedule, and removes the pen from the spine before opening it. "Nineteen Eighty-Nine." He says softly. "We have had to wait longer before, I suppose." He notes the year on the day and writes Paris. He folds it shut and drops it back in the drawer. He grabs a donut and lays back, looking up, wondering if Michael is looking down.

Leviathan

Leviathan stands in the Empty Realm, it still hasn't been cleared of the mess. Dead plants still line the floors. "Leviathan, is it?"

"You must be Gabriel." Leviathan turns, looking into angelic eyes. "How is the High Commander?"

"Alive, and the Crown?" Gabriel walks in, looking at the abandoned room.

"Also alive." Gabriel nods at that answer, stuffing his hands in his pockets.

"So what now?" Leviathan asks, sitting on the edge of the table that had been for Hell's council.

Gabriel pulls a piece of paper from his pocket

and hands it to Leviathan, who takes it tentatively and opens it. "Death sent this to us yesterday," He shakes his head, "Death killed Nergal for contempt of court."

Leviathan reads the letter before looking up at the angel. "Shall we call this ordeal settled then?"

"We shall." Gabriel nods. "Death said that Beelzebub tried to stop Nergal, which tells us your side was acting in good faith. That's enough for me."

"Aye, agreed." Leviathan hands him back the note. "Hopefully, this is the last we see one another."

Gabriel nods, looking him up and down but does extend his hand. Leviathan takes it, and shakes it. "Agreed. When Michael fully recovers, there are revisions to the treaties he would like to see enacted. Please get in touch with us at your soonest convenience when your leader is well. Good day and God bless." Gabriel takes back his hand and vanishes.

Leviathan sighs and looks around. He has somewhere he needs to be. He closes his eyes, and when they open, he's standing just beside the river near the waterfall. It's dawn. The sun is rising in the east, and the air is cool.

He walks to the edge of the water, looking up at the falls as they pour down into the river below. "It's still so beautiful." Raphael's voice catches him off guard, and he jumps, turning. "I didn't mean to scare you."

Leviathan rights himself and smooths out his jacket. "I am not frightened." He feigns, "Merely at your service." He takes the angel's hands in his own, leaning down to kiss knuckles. "How is your brother?" Gabriel had said, but he wanted to hear this from Raphael.

"Well, he's back up and running," a deep sigh. "Against my wishes. And your brother, Beelzebub?"

"Still unconscious, last I knew," Leviathan says softly. "But they expect him to wake soon."

"Did you speak with Gabriel?" Raphael asks. "I knew you were supposed to at some point today."

"Aye, moments ago, and we came to an agreement that it's over. Once Beelzebub and Michael are healed, they may wish to speak and come to terms over their contracts."

"That's diplomatic of Gabriel." Raphael snorts.

"He did not sound as though the ideas were of his design." Leviathan runs his fingers through

Raphael's hair. "Enough of Gabriel, speak no more of his wills. I have until dusk reaches New York to return to the throne to allow my sister her rest."

Raphael leans into his kiss, and they hold one another. "I have a few hours." He admits.

Leviathan beams as they turn their eyes up to the Moon, which still appears in the morning sky. "Tis beautiful."

"I know you said not to talk about him, but the Moon, that's Gabriel's, you know? He made it, something to do with your waters."

"Tides, yes." Leviathan sighs, "Perhaps we are of a kind Gabriel and me."

"I would like to think you could get along if he could look past your....everything."

Leviathan snorts but goes quiet with consideration. He has a few things on his mind. Some questions but something else. "Would you swim with me?" He backs up and pulls his bandolier off, dropping it and his sword to the ground. He starts to kick off his boots. He pulls his pistol free of its sheath and drops it onto his shoes.

"In the water?"

Leviathan chuckles, "Yes, it's where one swims." He shrugs. "I beg of you this kindness."

Raphael walks forward. Their feet are bare as he pushes up into the water. "You talk about the tide-"

Leviathan pulls his leather coat off, dropping it over his boots. "'Twas the ocean, my love, this is a river." He motions, "A current it has, but I shall not allow it to take you." He smiles and pulls his shirt off, dropping it down to the pile he's making. "Come." He extends a hand. "I shall not let you go."

Raphael looks around before pulling away from the outer layer of his robes, leaving just an expansive skirt below. He heaves a breath. "If I hate this."

Leviathan is already getting into the water. "You won't."

"If I do."

"You will not." Leviathan reaches for him. "For I will be with thee, to hold thee, protect thee-"

Raphael kisses him again, and he pulls the angel into the water. "It's freezing!"

Leviathan touches the water for a moment, and it warms slightly. "Apologies, the chills of the depths do not alert me so. One is used to the cold and the pressure of those depths."

Raphael is clinging to him. "This is insanity."

"Madness? No." Leviathan smiles and kisses him again. "Tis such a joy."

Raphael's golden eyes seem to glow in the low light. "Leviathan?"

"What is your will?" He says in a whisper.

"What happens if someone catches us? Like a watcher?"

"If we were to be caught and found to be worth destruction, I will follow you into nothingness."

Raphael doesn't speak. He looks around as they float, holding onto each other. "Raphael?"

"I don't want to think about losing you." Raphael says, "Now that I've just found you." He shakes his head. "No, we'll find a way."

Leviathan smiles at him. "Perhaps, angelic one, perhaps."

"Secrets aren't exactly lying."

"And what will you say if someone asks what you did tonight?"

"Me? That I saw the waterfall, that I went swimming, that I saw the Moon, and that I- found it all rather easy to love."

"Such beautiful truths," Leviathan murmurs against Raphael's neck.

"Let's hope they are good enough for Heaven."
Raphael chuckles and kisses him.

Leviathan smiles. "I'm sure, they are."

XIX

Beelzebub

Beelzebub, Crown Prince of Hell, accepts a room key at the front desk of L'Hotel Eden. The year of our Lord? 1989. The woman is kind and smiles, passing the key over to him. "To dial the front desk, you press zero; to dial out, you press 9." He smiles at her.

"Thanks." he motions to her, "I have a room service order I'd like sent up as soon as possible." He reaches into his jacket and slides the small note over to her.

She takes the paper and glances at it. "I'll send

it to the kitchen at once; if we cannot find the wine you have here, may we substitute?"

"Yes," Beelzebub says., "Of course, whatever you need to do."

"It'll be up within the hour." She walks away, and Beelzebub turns.

Michael is standing near the fountain in the lobby and has his hair cut relatively short but long enough that the horseshoe behind his ear isn't noticeable. It's a handsome look. Beelzebub walks over, Michael already walking to him. When they meet, Beelzebub smiles at him. "We have four days to negotiate the changes in the treaties."

Michael reaches up to pull the tortoiseshell glasses off his eyes and put them in the pocket of his jacket. "We do." He smiles. "It's good to see you."

"Four days." Beelzebub says excitedly, "We've never had four days."

"Let's not waste a moment, shall we?" Michael extends his elbow, and Beelzebub takes his arm; they walk together to the lift.

"People are staring." Beelzebub laughs.

"I don't care," Michael says and waves a finger, everyone around them going back to whatever it was they were doing before, the two of them now forgotten.

"Now, who's the one manipulating minds?" Beelzebub laughs as they enter the lift. "You gave me such shit five years ago."

"Someone told me five years ago that I should live a little." Michael laughs.

"Smart guy." Beelzebub boasts.

"That he is; I love him very much," Michael says once the doors on the lift close and their mouths join, Beelzebub moans into the kiss. "Are we in the Penthouse again? Is that what you reserved for us?"

"I'm never renting any other room." Beelzebub nods, holding up the key. Michael takes it, and they teleport into the Penthouse. Michael doesn't wait to start unbuttoning Beelzebub's shirt.

"Our room?" Michael says softly.

"Our Home," Beelzebub murmurs. "Ours, for as long as it's around."

"Beelzebub, you are my home," Michael says firmly. "This place in existence or not."

Beelzebub scoffs. "Sentimental-" he reaches up to unhook his tie.

"Something like that." Michael pulls off his jacket and lays it on one of the chairs before opening the french doors to the bedroom. "I love it here."

"Just need a kitchen," Beelzebub says softly.

"For your food?"

"Yes, what else would it be for?" Beelzebub laughs.

"We can plant that suggestion in the owner's head, and he'll think it was his idea, to remodel them." Michael nods, "Just as we would like it."

Beelzebub chuckles. "I think you're doing more than living a little there, Mike."

Michael opens the french doors to the bedroom and smiles at the sunlight streaming through the windows. "Four days, can I keep you in bed that long?" He looks back, golden eyes glittering, "Or is that too much to ask?"

Beelzebub scoffs and turns away to fight the blush on his face. "We do have to work; this is a work trip."

"I think everything we want to accomplish with this meeting we already accomplished on our calls. I'm thrilled Hell got a landline."

"It is rather nice to call you in the middle of the night." Michael's hands run up his neck and into his dark hair before grasping a handful and pulling Beelzebub's neck back gently. "Is there something you want, High Commander?" Beelzebub chuckles.

Michael kisses him silently. The kiss breaks, and the angel releases him, motioning to the bed, "I got you a gift." a motion to the bed.

Beelzebub has never been happier in his entire existence. There is a white box with a red bow. "Oh!" he laughs a little, lifting it in his hands, "I didn't get you anything."

"You brought yourself; that's all the gift I need."

Beelzebub snorts but pulls the ribbon off the box and lifts the lid. Inside the box is a black object. "What is this?"

"It's a pager." Michael says, "It's a new technology. We are giving them to all the angels. We page them when we want them to return to Heaven." he nods. "I have one too, well that's not entirely true, I have two, one for Heaven and one for you."

"How does it work?" Beelzebub looks at the clip on it and smiles.

"When I call a phone number, it'll show up on your pager. You know my Heavenly desk line." Michael smiles, motioning to the tiny screen. "You'll know to meet me here."

"And if I can't meet with you?" Beelzebub asks, "What do I do then?"

Michael sits on the edge of the bed. "You call my pager. If I don't hear from you within an hour, I'll know you'll meet me."

Beelzebub smiles, "No more couriers."

"No more couriers." Michael agrees. "So you see my number show up, you meet me if you can't, you send me a page back."

"This is amazing," Beelzebub says, turning it over.

"It is, and I did it because-" Michael stands. "I love you."

Beelzebub nods and puts the pager back in the box, grabbing Michael by his tie and pulling him into a kiss. "You wanna show me just how much you do, handsome?"

"Oh yes, your highness, I certainly do." Michael beams at him.

Beelzebub would never tell anyone this, of course, but for being damned, his life is sure starting to feel like Heaven.

When they emerge from the bedroom hours later, the food has gone cold, and the ice in the wine bucket has melted. Beelzebub sits down in a fluffy white robe on the sofa and looks at the cookies on a smaller plate, grabbing one to nibble on. "Ah, we missed dinner." Michael groans trying to straighten out his blonde hair.

"We were doing negotiations."

Michael beams at him, "Is that what we are gonna call that?"

"I dunno." Beelzebub laughs, but it dies. After a long silent moment, he speaks again, quieter, "Where do you think Death took Nergal?"

He knows this comes from nowhere, but it's been a few years, and he feels they need to cover it. Michael stands in his boxers at the bar, grabbing a few grapes out of a bowl. "I'm not sure," he says, popping a few in his mouth. "We know he can't be dead." he chews, coming back toward Beelzebub.

"He's no longer in my Legion," Beelzebub admits.

"You're not his host?"

"No." Beelzebub shakes his head, "I can't summon him, and we know he isn't dead. Like Death made Heaven and Hell believe."

"Death removed your mark from him. He has to still be with Death." Michael says, coming over to sit behind Beelzebub and pulling him to lay back against him. "Death said he would look after him."

"And we have each other," Beelzebub says softly. "Do we know anything about how or even when it will happen?"

"I've been going over things in the Heavenly library. From my understanding, we'll be summoned, called to service." Michael shrugs. "That our steads will seek us out, and we will ride to where the final battle is to be."

"Like horses?" Beelzebub frowns, "Farm beasts?"

"Horseman is a literal term, my love." Michael eats another grape and shrugs. "It talked about how our will would not be our own. We won't be able to stop it." Beelzebub thinks about that for a long while and sighs. "I'm the first to go." He says softly. "I'll be summoned first."

"Why you?"

"It's the start of a War, Bee." He leans down, kissing Beelzebub's hair. "I'm the herald of War. Then you will be summoned, and the humans will start to starve, hybrids too." he looks over, "Then plague will cover the land, and then death will sweep in and remove all souls bound for Heaven."

"The rapture," Beelzebub says softly.

"Yup." Michael nods. "And we won't be able to stop it when it happens, and I certainly won't know when it happens, but once I go, you'll know when it starts."

"How will I know?"

"I have entrusted a will to my brother Metatron." He murmurs. "Once I'm compromised, it contains my final wishes, and one of those is to warn Hell that it has begun."

"Give me time to try to hide or ...something."

"It'll come for you, and you can't hide from it. Delay it taking you maybe, but in the end, it will get you, Beelzebub." Michael sighs, "Like it will get Nergal, and like it will get Death too."

"But how does it start?"

"It says that the son of the morning star will break the seal of War," he says softly. "That he will be a horseman as well, that he will be one of great Conquest."

"So there's five of us?" Beelzebub sighs. He knows Lucifer had a son and knows where that son is too, another deal made with Death. "Shit." He doesn't say those things, not now. "And you said we won't know when it will happen?"

"The books don't say when, love; they just tell

what happens, not when it starts." Michael pulls him closer. "Could be tomorrow, could be a thousand years from now, we don't know."

"I hate not knowing," Beelzebub says and takes another cookie off the tray.

"I know." Michael rubs his arms. "Me too."

Beelzebub smiles at him. "We should go to a movie."

"I've never been to a cinema. Raphael went to one a few weeks ago, and he said it was wonderful." Michael seems receptive to the idea.

"My brother Leviathan enjoys them as well." He smiles. "Or we could stay in."

Michael sits up and turns Beelzebub to kiss him deeply. "I don't care." the Archangel says, "As long as I'm with you."

Beelzebub takes his hand and nods. "I couldn't have said it better myself."

XX

Epilogue: Death

Nergal stands next to the water and looks as if it flows seemingly in both directions. "This will be your job now." Death says to him, "You will not remember; no one will know you, and you will work for me."

"It'll keep me from getting anyone sick?" Death can see the worry on the demon's face.

"Yes, you won't have contact with humans." Death says, "You will be my ferryman and take souls to Heaven and Hell for deliveries." He gestures around.

"I can't get into Heaven. I'm a demon." Nergal says, "Unless you can change that too."

"I cannot change that. You can drop the deliveries off at their gates." Death says softly. "It will make sense soon, child. You won't even consider not being able to enter the gates."

Nergal looks around and nods. "Sure, why not?" He looks back into Death's shroud with a shrug, "Not like I have a host of other options waiting for me."

Death touches his face. "It cannot be destroyed, only repurposed." A mantra.

The being in front of him changes, wings glittering gray. "Who, who are you?"

Death turns around. "I am Death." He murmurs.

"Do I have a name?" He asks softly, brightly, eagerly.

"I give you the name Bartholomew." Death says kindly. "You have your instructions." He motions to the ferry. "Your work begins now."

Bartholomew smiles and turns to the little boat. "Yes, sir!" He grabs the oar and goes down the small dock to the little boat, its hold already full.

Death watches as Bartholomew use the oar and pushes off the dock.

Hundreds

Once Bartholomew is out of sight, Death nods. "Until such a time as the call to service comes for us both, you will be in service to me, brother." Death turns away, leaving the ferryman on his boat.

THE END

Acknowledgements

Cover: Angels Party Flyer Template V3 | Free posters design for photoshop. (n.d.). *That's Design Store* Retrieved Feb 10, 2021, from https://www.thatsdesignstore.com/product/angels-party-flyer-template-v3/

Free image on Pixabay-House Fly- Fly, Insect, Flies, Pest. (n.d.). Retrieved Feb 10th, 2021, from HTTPs://pixabay.com/vectors/house-fly-fly-insect-files-pest-24629/

Halloween Flyer Poster Template PSD Customizable with photoshop V28 (n.d.). *That's Design Store* Retrieved Feb 10, 2021, from https://www.thatsdesignstore.com/product/halloween-flyer-template-v28/

Copyright

www.ingramcontent.com/pod-product-compliance
Lightning Source LLC
Chambersburg PA
CBHW060918140726
47996CB00001B/291